THE
REAL FOOD DAILY
COOKBOOK

THE REAL FO

OD DAILY

REALLY FRESH, REALLY GOOD, REALLY VEGETARIAN

COOKBOOK

ANN GENTRY

WITH ANTHONY HEAD

TEN SPEED PRESS
Berkeley | Toronto

Ten Speed Press
Box 7123
Berkeley, California 94707
www.tenspeed.com

Distributed in Australia by Simon and Schuster Australia, in Canada by Ten Speed Press Canada, in New Zealand by Southern Publishers Group, in South Africa by Real Books, and in the United Kingdom and Europe by Airlift Book Company.

Cover and text design by Toni Tajima
Food styling by Ronnda Hamilton
Photography assistance by Craig Wadlin

Library of Congress Cataloging-in-Publication Data
Gentry, Ann, 1954–
    The Real Food Daily cookbook : really fresh, really good, really vegetarian / Ann Gentry with Anthony Head.
       p. cm.
    Includes index.
    ISBN-13: 978-1-58008-618-9 (pbk.)
    ISBN-10: 1-58008-618-7 (pbk.)
    1. Vegetarian cookery. 2. Real Food Daily (Restaurant) I. Head, Anthony, 1968– II. Title.
TX837.G393 2005
    641.5'636—dc22   2005016245

Printed in China
First printing, 2005

1 2 3 4 5 6 7 8 9 10 — 09 08 07 06 05

Contents

Acknowledgments

Much appreciation to my agent Bob Silverstein at Quicksilver Books for his encouragement and patience.

Thanks to all the folks at Ten Speed Press for their interest and enthusiasm about the book. My gratitude to Lorena Jones who put me in the hands of Meghan Keeffe and Toni Tajima. Thank you ladies for shaping the book and making it something I am proud of. Also, thanks to Jessica Boone for capturing the spirit of Real Food Daily in her photographs.

A warm thanks to Rochelle Palermo, who has a great sense of humor, a true love for food, and an unfaltering willingness to keep trying until it's right. Also thanks to her husband and grandmother who tasted many of the recipes and always loved them.

To Anthony Head, your steady calmness kept me sane when I started to feel uncertain about my ideas. You took my memories, ramblings, and streams of consciousness and made sense out of them. You've shaped my words to hopefully inspire and educate others.

Thank you to Karen Claffey, Miquel Martinez, Tom Hartwell, David Anderson, Jose Aramayo, Britt Hawley, and all the other talented and energetic culinary people who have made creative contributions to the menu and the success of Real Food Daily.

Thank you to my staff whose hard work and dedication make it happen daily.

Many thanks to John Kaufman who has supported my vision and helped me raise the standards of excellence in my restaurants. It's been an amazing journey.

I am especially grateful to my husband, Robert Jacobs, for his passion and steadfast belief in what I do. His direction and input have been invaluable to my growth as a restaurateur. What a process this has been!

My gratitude to my shareholders who "put their money where their mouths are."

And finally, a loving thank-you to my family of loyal customers who have been coming to Real Food Daily since the beginning, and to the thousands of other people who have walked through the doors. Your support and patronage has allowed me to present real food to the world. It has been an honor to serve you.

Welcome

When I opened Real Food Daily (RFD) twelve years ago, I made a commitment to serve a menu free of animal products and featuring certified organic produce. I'm proud that I've stuck to that commitment through the opening of two additional restaurants. When I started out, so many people told me that I couldn't do it. Who would come to a restaurant, they asked, that only served plant-based cuisine? "You should at least put a little fish and chicken on the menu" was the well-intentioned advice I got most often. (I won't even tell you what was said when they found out I wasn't going to use white sugar or dairy fats in my baked goods.)

Deep down inside of me, I knew I could prove them wrong—although that wasn't my motivation at that time, and it's still not what drives me today. I just knew that people were looking for this kind of food but didn't know where to get it. I also knew that the type of food RFD served would nurture people on so many important levels that they would want to come back again and again. They did— and they still do.

My restaurants have surpassed my wildest dreams, and not just in the double-digit sales growth every year but, more important, in the variety of people dining with us. I'd comfortably say that over half of our guests are not vegetarian or vegan. Instead, they're simply educated consumers who want high-quality ingredients prepared in creative and innovative ways. They want food that is delicious and satisfying. They want *real food*.

This cookbook continues Real Food Daily's culinary journey. It's for vegetarians, vegans, and everyone else. The recipes are perfect for beginning an expedition into healthful eating, or just for finding something delicious for dinner. And whether for health or ethical reasons, philosophical or environmental concerns, more people are turning toward a plant-based diet. My team and I continue to dedicate ourselves to raising the standards and expectations for this style of cooking, incorporating exciting flavors from around the world to create meals that are incomparable in taste, texture, and satisfaction.

You don't have to be vegan or vegetarian to love this type of cooking. Simply put, this book is for everyone who loves good food.

My Story

Others in my business will tell you they were wowed by food from an early age and spent their formative years cooking in the kitchen with Mom. Maybe they sold their homemade brownies for a dime in grammar school before moving on to be classically trained in the culinary arts at Le Cordon Bleu or the Culinary Institute of America. For them, food has been front and center nearly all their lives.

But that's just not the case with me.

My interest in food developed much later in life and was a natural outgrowth of who I was at the time and where I was heading. But that's not to say I didn't grow up surrounded by good food. As a girl in Memphis, Tennessee, I always enjoyed plenty of freshly baked biscuits, home-cooked vegetables, and, yes, even peach pies cooling on the windowsill.

But the era of the late 1950s and 1960s was a unique time in American kitchen history because the advances in food technology really began squeezing out the made-from-scratch style of cooking. My mother, who was raising two kids by herself, worked a lot and increasingly had less time to put together such elaborate meals. That meant we shopped at gargantuan new supermarkets loaded with frozen, processed, and canned foods. We also ate our fair share of restaurant

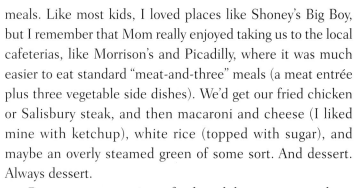

meals. Like most kids, I loved places like Shoney's Big Boy, but I remember that Mom really enjoyed taking us to the local cafeterias, like Morrison's and Picadilly, where it was much easier to eat standard "meat-and-three" meals (a meat entrée plus three vegetable side dishes). We'd get our fried chicken or Salisbury steak, and then macaroni and cheese (I liked mine with ketchup), white rice (topped with sugar), and maybe an overly steamed green of some sort. And dessert. Always dessert.

But even as convenience foods and the restaurant culture spread throughout the South and the rest of the country, my mother's side of the family held firm to their kitchen roots.

My maternal grandmother ("Maw Maw") and my aunt Ann Eliz-
abeth Dawson (whom I was named after) were quite accomplished cooks who cherished their handed-down family recipes
and spent most days—and *all* day at that—in the kitchen. They
still believed in making everything from scratch and used only
high-quality ingredients.

They also believed in etiquette, so I remember sitting down to
their dinner table with pressed cloth napkins, fine china, and pol-
ished silverware—it was a proper southern spread every time. I was
taught excellent table manners and I was expected to demonstrate
them at every meal. It was only right, considering how much work
went into making those elaborate, delicious meals. Looking back, I
feel blessed that I could be a part of that world—a world filled with
the smells, the sounds, and the art of cooking and dining.

But cooking wasn't high on my list of passions when I left home for college,
deciding instead that I wanted to be an actress. A few years after leaving Memphis,
I was in New York City, working in theater off-Broadway and waiting tables. It
seemed as though New York was food, food, food, everywhere. Exciting restaurants
were opening all the time, the nightlife didn't quit until the sun came up, and I was
fortunate to be surrounded by some of the most interesting people on the planet—
people like Roger Leggat, one of the cooks at Whole Wheat and Wild Berries, one
of the leading vegetarian restaurants in Greenwich Village, where I waited tables.

Everybody loved Roger. He was a gentle man with an incredible passion for life.
Even though he wasn't a trained chef, he took me to open-air markets and taught me
how to pick out the best fresh produce and then how to treat it right in the kitchen.
He presented food in a very beautiful, sensual way. (You can bet I showed my best
manners at his table. Just like my family, he earned my respect.) Maybe I wasn't
consciously paying attention to everything, but I was soaking up all this culinary
information for later in life when I would have my own proper kitchen—and for
when I would eventually open a restaurant and carry on what Roger taught me.

Besides learning about how food was grown and prepared, for the first time I
was also learning what healthful foods were all about. Some of my best teachers
were the people I waited on. It was a very impressionable time for me as many

exciting and fascinating people filled my tables and shared their stories of how changing their diets changed their lives. Within months, I embraced vegetarianism.

Cutting out animal products helped establish my commitment to better health. But even as a vegetarian I still craved sugar and caffeine, both of which affected my moods and overall health. I was a "junk-food vegetarian"—my term for someone who doesn't eat a balanced meatless diet.

As exciting as life was, I just didn't feel that good most of the time. I was constantly riding the sugar roller coaster, and I found myself worn down from waiting tables, auditioning, and acting around the clock. I became very sick from what I later came to understand was just an imbalance in my life and my diet (it is usually both), and after several rounds of the traditional Western treatment of antibiotics, I still wasn't well. In a moment of desperation—or enlightenment, depending on how you look at it—I decided to take the radical step of fasting on brown rice and miso soup. On that limited but powerfully nutritious diet, it didn't take long for my infection to heal and my strength to return.

That's when I really started to observe a connection between the food I ate and the way I felt. Shortly after that, I was introduced to macrobiotics. This Asian approach to eating (and life in general) was influencing many people throughout New York, and I learned all I could about it. I went to macrobiotic restaurants and workshops and learned how to be in tune with my surroundings, the seasons, and what was on my plate; and I learned how to use foods medicinally. The power of this lesson is the foundation of Real Food Daily's approach to eating today. (For more about macrobiotics, see the section When East Meets West.)

Perhaps the most important aspect of embracing this dietary and lifestyle philosophy was that I felt compelled to start cooking for myself. In the beginning, I admit, I was a lousy cook. But the funny thing about really committing to a task—especially an unfamiliar one—is learning to accept the screwups that come fast, frequently, and without mercy. Overcooking, undercooking, burning, sloppy cutting techniques—I did them all. But I reminded myself to have patience, and my passion for what I was doing helped me stick it out and eventually become a pretty good home cook.

I had a great support system at that time. My friends Ellen Goldsmith and Thalia Christo were also very interested in macrobiotic cooking. Ellen was my very best friend during my twenties, and we threw potluck dinners and saw what dishes other friends in our circle had mastered. Thalia was my next-door neighbor, and she already had excellent kitchen skills since she'd cooked professionally. We had many discussions on what was supposed to be happening in the kitchen versus what was actually happening.

This was also the time when I started to imagine that I could really open a restaurant of my own someday, a place that served my own version of vegetarian cuisine. Nevertheless, I was still focused on my acting career, which is why I left New York for Los Angeles in 1986.

With California's year-round growing season, I was expecting to discover a mecca of natural foods restaurants when I arrived. But I could find only two such places serving the balanced, healthful cuisine I loved, and, wouldn't you know it, one of them closed right after I arrived.

I kept cooking for myself, and whenever I brought my home-cooked meals to the set, people would ooh and aah and request samples. To accommodate this growing demand for my food, I began setting up a proper kitchen in my apartment and realized how many great kitchen tools there were to make quick work of so many tasks. And shopping at farmers' markets for organic ingredients was totally rewarding in terms of cost, variety, and abundance.

As my cooking reputation grew, I had the opportunity to work as Danny DeVito's private chef while he directed and acted in *Throw Mama from the Train*. (He was expecting a professional, so I guess you could say that this was perhaps my greatest acting role—starring as a professional caterer.) I cooked full-time for three months in Danny's Winnebago and created many great recipes—some I still make to this day. Just as important, I took my cooking skills to the professional level.

When the gig ended, I was confident that I could turn my one-woman operation into something larger, and I just knew there had to be more people out there who were searching for this kind of food. I started a home-delivery service for a small but very enthusiastic group of customers. I was fulfilled because I was influencing people's lives in a very positive way. They relied on my food service to help get them through their days, whether they were parents feeding the kids healthful, balanced meals or hardworking singles who wanted to come home to a well-cooked dinner. Then one day while I was driving up the Malibu coast, the words "real food every day" popped into my head, and the next thing I knew, I was eating, drinking, and sleeping the Real Food Daily business.

I was still acting, but when my private customer base reached over thirty people a day, it was clear that I had to make a tough choice. It was a deeply personal decision, but ultimately I chose to pursue what was giving me such an enormous amount of satisfaction. I graciously said good-bye to my acting career. Within twenty-four hours I was working on a new mission: to open a restaurant serving the vegan dishes I had been perfecting for years.

It was during this time that two very special men entered my life. Well, one re-entered my life: Roger Leggat showed up on the West Coast and gave me the beautiful gift of working with me in the kitchen on the day-to-day operations of

the home-delivery service while I devoted more time to getting the plans for a restaurant under way. Also, my future husband, Robert Jacobs, became one of my customers, and he was in the retail business. When I told him of my plans to open a restaurant, he helped me put together a business plan, and together we started to make my dream come true.

At that time, I knew I wanted to make one more bold move with my cooking. I wanted to feature a vegan menu, using as many organic and locally grown products as I could get my hands on. Although it would be difficult, I knew these were ways to make my restaurant stand apart from other vegetarian restaurants. You see, I wanted to be a different kind of restaurateur—someone who cared about the nurturing aspect of food as much as I cared about running a successful business. I trusted my intuition that people would come for this food as long as I could nourish them and provide them with good service.

The first Real Food Daily restaurant opened in 1993 in Santa Monica, California, and it never would have happened without the support, knowledge, and love of so many friends and family members along the way. Looking back today, with three restaurants successfully up and running and more on the way, I fully realize that I was taught that food should always be served with care and love. I certainly haven't forgotten my southern roots when it comes to cooking today—both for my family and for my customers. If it doesn't taste good and if it doesn't satisfy, then it's just not *real* food.

Real Food Daily Profile

When I welcome new employees to Real Food Daily, I like to tell them that I'm honored to be the person who walks with the history. As the founder of RFD, I have seen firsthand the impact of what we have accomplished for more than twelve years. From day one, Real Food Daily has proven to be exceptionally popular no matter where we go.

I can still vividly recall the day the first restaurant opened. It was the summer solstice, June 21, 1993. We swung wide our doors to the oceanside community of Santa Monica, California, and—with no advertising—over one hundred people showed up. They were both stunned at how beautiful and inviting our space was and excited about the food we served. It was a true thrill to see such support, and it confirmed what I thought all along: there were so many people searching for this pure, clean-tasting food.

Our menu was much smaller than it is today. Because of the rice, beans, and sea vegetables, people pegged us as a macrobiotic restaurant. They were right to some extent, but that wasn't the whole picture at all. I took what I knew about macrobiotics and combined it with contemporary notions of vegan cuisine to create something truly unique. What we were really serving (not to be found anywhere else) was a new concept of comfort food that didn't lack the excitement and taste of more mainstream foods. It made you feel good and it was delicious.

From the beginning, we always made most of our food from scratch right in the restaurant and always chose fresh, high-quality organic ingredients to work with. Along with developing comprehensive seasonal menus that appealed to so many guests, our creativity really shined with the daily specials, soups, and desserts, always giving our diners delicious reasons to return.

We also prided ourselves on our friendly and educated staff, who took the time to get to know our returning guests. Our service and hospitality have always been key elements to the organization, because at our heart we are a neighborhood restaurant. We are an anchor to the community, providing a nurturing environment. Our customers trust us and respect the fact that they know what they're getting at Real Food Daily.

We had been open for only seven months when a severe earthquake hit in January 1994. No one at our location was hurt, but the building's parapet fell into

rubble in front of the restaurant. It took four months for us to clean up the mess inside and out, and all the while we were inundated with phone calls, handwritten messages, and business cards left at the front door asking us to spread the word when we reopened. We got up and running again, but for more than a year our storefront windows were covered with a wooden façade and scaffolding while construction continued all around us. I like to look back at that challenging time as a testament to our staying power. Not only did we bounce back stronger than ever, but we fed a lot of the construction workers and did our own little part to rebuild our neighborhood and make it better than ever. With the Santa Monica location firmly established, we opened our second location in West Hollywood in 1998. It was fascinating to me because this neighborhood had a different vibe altogether. Our location put us on a long stretch of road known around Los Angeles as "Restaurant Row" because of its many expensive, nationally recognized restaurants. And yet this neighborhood embraced us with open arms and hungry stomachs. That spurred us on to even greater innovation in the kitchen.

In 2003, we opened the third Real Food Daily, in Beverly Hills. Another new neighborhood and another new crowd. Once again, it was demonstrated quite plainly that people were searching for creative and delicious organic vegan food.

Our continued success tells me that vegan cuisine's time has come and that it stacks up next to any food on the planet. Not only is our food accepted as a healthful alternative to the standard American diet, but with our imagination and creativity in the kitchen, it's also one of the most exciting cuisines to have developed over the past ten years.

Who We Are Today

When we first opened in 1993, the word *vegan* was out there on the fringe. (In fact, the concept that vegetarian dining could be healthful was just barely taking hold.) But today, vegan ideals are much more accepted. Nutrition science backs up the healthfulness of meatless diets, and, more important, the growing number of people who enjoy vegan meals—at least occasionally—is indisputable.

As we continue to gain momentum and expand our business, we at Real Food Daily are proud that we still have guests who have been with us from the very beginning. Every day, we buck the notion that meatless dining is obscure, tasteless food served in a bland atmosphere. And because our cuisine has such universal appeal, our loyal customers are not limited to die-hard vegans—not by a long shot, in fact. The health-conscious diners and the part-time vegetarians mix seamlessly in our dining rooms with the epicurean experts. (This is Los Angeles, after all, where the culinary climate is world-class.)

Our second decade represents growth and expansion in two ways. For one thing, we're bringing this food to a mainstream audience and ushering in a modern appreciation for this smart way of eating. And we're also taking this cuisine to new heights with the fusion of exotic and flavorful ingredients from around the world. A Real Food Daily kitchen is an artistic arena where inspiration and creation come together to produce stunning dishes for contemporary tastes.

From the beginning, we had the media spotlight on us, and it continues to shine brightly today. We've been featured in publications like *Bon Appétit, Cooking Light, VegNews, Fit, InStyle,* and many other local and national publications, and we appear often on the Food Network. Why, even as this cookbook was being put together, our vegan burger (page 126) was named one of the Top Five Burgers in Los Angeles by Citysearch.

We've grown from just contributing to a niche market to being an industry leader. So many diet trends have come and gone, and although we love to update our dishes with delicious new offerings, we have never altered our menu to match a fad diet. That's because you can't go wrong with fresh, seasonal, organic, and plant-based food. While others are counting carbs, calories, and fat grams, we remain focused on the food. We've stayed true to what we know—and that's the reason for this cookbook.

When East Meets West

In the past few decades, the tremendous strides in Western medicine have been enhanced by greater acceptance of Eastern healing traditions that treat the body and mind as equal partners in wellness. Yoga, meditation, and acupuncture are obvious examples of Asian practices that are more common in our society today as people look for alternative paths to better health. Innovative approaches to nutrition are not to be overlooked either.

Time-honored theories of nutrition from China state that different foods affect different systems and organs of the body. An excess or deficiency of a food or food group can sometimes lead to illness. With these views in mind, it becomes important to recognize food as medicine, capable of healing as much as nurturing. But that doesn't mean that you should treat food as you would a pill. It's not to be taken *only* when something goes wrong. Nutrition is an ongoing and evolving program.

I feel that diet is a very personal choice and one that is almost exclusively within your control. While some people don't make the connection between what goes into your mouth and what comes out of your life, I believe that the link is undeniable.

Macrobiotics is a philosophy of life that encourages us to always be conscious of the big picture while creating a physical, mental, and spiritual balance for health and happiness. The practice was brought to the United States from Japan in 1959 by Michio Kushi and Herman Aiharia, and the philosophy immediately found a devoted following. I first began studying macrobiotics when I lived in New York City, and I found its principles made sense and, most important, made me feel much better inside and out. And my diet, I learned, is an important application of these principles to the natural order of my own personal environment.

Followers of macrobiotics believe in the principles of yin and yang, the opposite yet complementary natural forces that create an orderly universe. Macrobiotics classifies each food as yin or yang based on its relationship with other foods and according to a variety of factors, including where it was grown; its water content, color, taste, and texture; and its effect on the body.

Chinese five-element theory is also important in macrobiotics. According to this theory, everything in our physical world can be classified into five distinct but interconnected components: fire, wood, earth, water, and metal. Traditional

Chinese medicine relies on five-element theory to explain the relationships among the body organs and tissues, as well as between the body and its surrounding physical environment.

Here's how five-element theory applies to nutrition: When translated to foods, the five elements are classified as bitter, sour, sweet, salty, and pungent. Since these are the primary tastes your tongue experiences, incorporating the five elements into your meals means that you're going to feel satisfied. Creating this kind of balance in your diet helps to balance your body—and that puts you in harmony with your environment.

I want to stress that *this is not a macrobiotic cookbook*. I don't think there is one perfect way to eat, and I know that there is no miracle diet. But I have incorporated into this book many of the lessons I learned from my days developing recipes as a macrobiotic cook. The dishes here are filled with whole grains, vegetables, legumes, and soy products. They're high in unrefined carbohydrates and fiber while being naturally low in fat—but there's nothing fanatical about that.

Western medicine now stresses eating a more plant-based diet to get the essential vitamins, minerals, antioxidants, and phytochemicals that are found abundantly—and in some cases exclusively—in the plant kingdom that surrounds us. These nutrients help to fight cancer, heart disease, and many other ailments in our bodies while nourishing and invigorating our lives. The Real Food Daily approach is an innovative and life-enhancing blend of world cuisines, and this book is about living in harmony with our environment and reaping the delicious rewards.

A Few Words on Eating with the Seasons

When I was growing up in Memphis, our family often drove north to my grandmother's house along a route dotted with roadside produce stands. We stopped so many times to grab something fresh to fix for dinner that the road felt like our very own grocery store. I remember asking one winter afternoon, "Where are the peaches?" The roadside farmer told me that peaches grow only in summer, and I guess the notion that there are certain foods for certain times of the year never left me.

These days, produce—peaches included—is available from all over the world, twenty-four hours a day, all year long. As much as that can be a culinary advantage, especially when you're in the middle of winter and craving, say, a juicy tomato for homemade salsa, remember that your body is on the seasonal clock, too.

I've learned a great deal about the body's inner clock through the practice of macrobiotics. One of the principles of this ancient Chinese science is to understand the connections among ourselves, the foods we eat, and the environment in which we live. Choosing local foods grown only in season completes this natural harmony while supporting the region. And by "local food" I mean any food grown in the same regional climate and environment as the one in which we live.

I've heard a unique perspective on seasonal foods from my friend Phil McGrath, who owns McGrath Farms in Camarillo, California. Phil delivers his fresh organic produce to my restaurants. He tells me that the will of the consumer is so strong that it forces farmers like him to push food out of its season. Even though strawberries, one of his specialties, have a short growing season (April to July is the very best time), he has demands for the fruit as late as September and even October. He can extend the season, and with economic conditions being what they are, he has to. But he tells me honestly that as far as taste, appearance, and texture are concerned, the strawberry you're getting in August or later is not going to taste as good as the one in June because it's simply not nature's time for strawberries.

As a restaurateur, I too understand consumer pressure. Every year my poor waitstaff takes some flack when we stop serving dishes that have gone out of season, like when we change the summer corn for the winter squash on the Real Food Meal. I could serve the squash right through summer, but at that time of year, it is grown in another hemisphere, refrigerated, and shipped in. Either vegetable wouldn't be as tasty or attractive as when it's fresh, and I don't feel it's healthy to serve it out of season.

Giving up some of our favorite foods for a few months requires a shift in our thinking—and lots of patience. Ultimately, though, I believe we are healthier and more balanced beings if we honor the seasons and stay true to the laws of nature. And just as surely as spring will come again, so, too, will all those marvelous ingredients.

A Few More Words on Eating Organically

As a mother, I choose organic foods because it just makes sense to give my family the freshest ingredients that were grown in harmony with nature rather than against it. My family is rewarded by its dedication, too. Research has shown that organically grown produce contains higher amounts of cancer-fighting antioxidants than food grown conventionally.

As a chef, I'm incredibly aware of flavors and how my diners react to them. So after more than a decade of working at the restaurants, I can say without a doubt that organic foods taste better than their conventionally grown counterparts. My customers will tell you that too, which is why 85 to 90 percent of the ingredients at Real Food Daily are certified organic.

I'm happy to see that huge agribusinesses have jumped on the organic bandwagon, helping raise the profile of sustainable agriculture, as well as helping to bring costs down. They make it possible for nearly everyone around the country to shop for organic foods. But I've also noticed that the family farmers who have been practicing these organic techniques for so long—because they're committed to sustainable farming and they don't agree with conventional farming practices—are getting lost in the shuffle. They are slowly being squeezed to the margins by the bigger farming conglomerates.

I want to tell you that you can find these great and dedicated people at your local farmers' markets. Not only do I encourage you to eat as many organic foods as you can, I'd also like to invite you to visit a farmers' market and get to know some of these people. Start up a conversation with them, find out how long they've been around, and ask them for their recommendations. Not only will you taste some of the freshest, most healthful food around, but you'll learn an awful lot about your community, its history, and its diversity.

A Guide to Real Food

On the surface, being a vegan does mean excluding some foods. But looking at the situation on a deeper level, vegan cooking opens up so many more avenues to flavor than you thought existed. For instance, there are countless varieties of rice and more chiles around the world than can be named here. Why, there are at least thirteen varieties of persimmons alone.

And because of the staggering numbers of ingredients that can be combined in vegan cuisine, you never have to repeat a dish—unless you fall in love with it, which happens all the time. You can always use the various flavorful components to create new offerings, be they side dishes, appetizers, or main courses.

Preparing Real Food at Home

The best news is that you don't have to become a gourmet chef to eat well at home. In fact, just learning a few basic kitchen skills allows you to expand and embellish your usual dining selections and make your meals more appealing and healthful. Some basic kitchen wisdom also allows you to be responsible for what you eat as opposed to always relying on others to feed you. In our world of fast-food restaurants, it's satisfying to know that you can put together a few meals for yourself and your family—and that they're going to taste better anyway.

Shopping

Sometimes you need to turn notions on their heads. Shopping is one such notion. While it's great to choose a recipe and go to the market with your list in hand, other times it's more fulfilling to do just the opposite: Let the produce inspire you. What's in season? What looks good? After getting to the grocery store—or better yet to the farmers' market—and seeing the vibrant red bell peppers, smelling the fresh and fragrant herbs, and maybe even tasting a succulent just-picked apricot, then decide what you're in the mood to make.

Some of the ingredients in these recipes may not be immediately recognizable to you. That's okay. Cooking is about discovery, and sometimes you have to get off the beaten path to find what you're looking for. It's worth your while, though, to visit natural foods stores, farmers' markets, and ethnic markets, where you'll find some of the more exotic ingredients. Since these markets are loaded with some of the most flavorful foods in the world, the end results will more than make up for the time you spend.

Confidence in the kitchen

As I continue to build my own kitchen skills, there are two basic principles that I think pretty much cover every possible situation that can arise: Stay Loose and Stay the Course. By "Stay Loose" I mean that at any level of cooking—beginner, weekend enthusiast, or master chef—you must accept that mistakes happen. Be flexible when they do. In my first five years of cooking, I clung tightly to this point because I felt there was always so much more to learn. Sometimes goof-ups lead to delicious discoveries. Sometimes they lead to calling your favorite neighborhood takeout. But remember that if you make a really bad mistake, it's just one meal and not the end of the world. Each kitchen session—good or bad—builds your repertoire of recipes and strengthens your cooking skills.

"Stay the Course" is my golden rule for remembering to follow the recipe. Over the years I've shared some of Real Food Daily's recipes with friends and customers, and I've received a few complaints about the results. When I ask about how they approached the recipe, inevitably I learn that they didn't use a certain ingredient or they left out a step or two to save time. Well, I say that you can't get to your destination unless you follow the road map. Always read the recipe from the first ingredient through the last cooking step *before* going into the kitchen. This reduces the chance of surprises when your hands are full of napa cabbage. Organize all the ingredients you'll be using so you'll have exactly what you need when you need it.

Also, have patience with the recipe. Sometimes certain steps take longer than expected, or they're more complex than you thought. Don't give up. Hang in there and complete the recipe. Once you've mastered a recipe and can make it in the dark, feel free to experiment with it. Just remember to stay loose when you do.

Creating moods

One of my favorite cookbooks, *The Self-Healing Cookbook*, was self-published by Kristina Turner in 1987 and continues to sell strongly to this day. No wonder: The book has a powerful message about using foods as a way to change your mood. I take that message a bit further by insisting that the mood you bring to the kitchen dictates what you and others get out of a meal. Going into the kitchen to prepare even a simple dish, I find it's helpful to be tuned in to where I am emotionally.

And while I've entered the kitchen in many different moods, I find it's best for me to consider the kitchen as a place of refuge, a place where I can give in to the rhythm of cooking—slow, precise, thoughtful. Personally, I sometimes find that I like to be in the kitchen by myself and accomplish the meal on my own. The act of cooking takes me away from the mental and physical places I've been in previously. Whether I'm dealing with my kids at home or spending all day at the restaurant, when I cook I love the solace that comes with it.

But there are also those times when I'm entertaining or the family meal gets really elaborate and creative and I find that I need more legs and more arms to get everything done. There is never any shortage of volunteers, and I never say no to friends and family who want to be in the kitchen, too. They want to participate. They want to help. So the kitchen becomes a festive gathering place—alive with energy. My point is to always be comfortable in the kitchen, and your mood will translate to the plate.

Timing

In cooking—as in finding love, buying a house, and so many other areas of life—timing is everything. And I'm not just referring to the amount of time on the clock it takes to cook and serve a meal. I'm talking about the ability to get everything to the table at the same time. I think this is part skill and part art form. The way you plan your meals before you start cooking is vital to success. So analyze your menu beforehand and chart the prep times and cooking times of each dish, right down to the tossing of the salad. Prep any dishes in advance that you can. Soon, the whole process will become second nature to you.

You definitely want to buy some time when preparing dishes that require marinating or complex preparation. If you are cooking for a large party, it will relieve the pressure if you prepare some dishes the day before.

Intuition

We are creatures of habit who often get stuck on cooking and eating a few foods all the time. I don't think that's particularly healthful, and I know it's not that much fun. For many years I've been guided in my dietary choices by some of the theories of Chinese medicine, especially balancing color, shape, texture, flavor, and the nutritional components of food on the plate. Through this practice, my health and my livelihood have benefited greatly from the wider variety of foods I eat.

And then there's taste. For the newly acquainted, serving salty, sweet, sour, pungent, and bitter foods for every meal—as macrobiotic guidelines emphasize—might be a bit of a challenge. But since different foods affect the body differently, and because the many essential nutrients our bodies need come wrapped in different packages, it's a good idea to start composing your meals with an eye for variety.

This is not hard to accomplish: Pickles or miso, for instance, are good and salty; sweet vegetables like winter squash contain naturally occurring sugars; lemons and limes add a delicious sour touch to meals; pungent leeks and watercress are exceptionally versatile ingredients; and asparagus and some leafy greens demonstrate how bitter can also be delicious. Start out by trying to eat something from each of these taste categories on a daily basis. (To make it even easier, let color guide you. Aim to eat something brown, orange, white, green, yellow, and red.) That way you're sure to get a balanced diet that satisfies on every level. As you become more accustomed to these guidelines, planning each meal with such exquisite variety will get much easier.

Incorporating leftovers and prepared foods

It's not uncommon for me to start planning tomorrow's meals while I'm cooking tonight's dinner. And while I am a great believer in putting together meals with freshly prepared food, that doesn't stop me from incorporating leftovers into a new meal. The brown rice I used in the nori maki today might find new life in the veggie stir-fry I make tomorrow. This helps save some time while not wasting perfectly good food. So wherever it's appropriate, I've included extra uses for the components of the recipes. I urge you to try out those suggestions to save yourself time and effort.

For those who don't have as much time as they'd like to spend in the kitchen (and at home I am one of them), I recommend making a meal using fresh ingredients for certain dishes and store-bought foods for a dish or two. Oftentimes, it is the prepared food that inspires the rest of the meal.

At the table

Remember those family meals in the dining room? Dinners were real feasts, real celebrations. Sometimes we lingered at the table for hours. Those were special times for me growing up, and I choose to create that atmosphere as often as possible for my family.

In your home, whether you're cooking for yourself, for your family, or for large parties, the meal becomes so much more than just food on the table when you take the time to serve it with style. But two minutes before the dinner bell rings is not the time to try to set the table with grace. Think about what the meal calls for when you're organizing your ingredients. Then choose cloth napkins, place settings, and an appropriate assortment of serving bowls or platters with serving spoons and forks.

When the food is ready, I love to put everything in the middle of the table so everyone can see the beauty of what I have created. Even when I eat by myself, I still follow this ritual. I enjoy not only the nurturing feelings, but also the sense of accomplishment. Such presentations add another dimension to the dining experience and make the dinner table a special gathering place for your family—a place where they'll want to spend more time. It may take a bit longer to clean up, but after you've presented such a wonderful meal, you're sure to find plenty of volunteers still lingering at the table.

Equipping Your Kitchen

As you can imagine, many professional chefs go to extremes at work, using nearly every kitchen tool, gadget, and gizmo ever created to make cooking speedy. When we're at home, you might be surprised to learn, we try to keep it simple—just like everyone else. That's because our kitchens are, for the most part, just like yours; somehow, there's never enough space.

Whether you live in a spacious home or a studio apartment, think about what makes sense when it comes to appliances, food storage, and counter space. Flip through design magazines, visit appliance showrooms, check out how and why your friends have things set up the way they do—and then create your own personal space that defines your personality. But remember: You're here to work, and the kitchen should be set up for efficiency as well as aesthetics.

Unless you're an appliance junkie, don't feel pressured to buy up everything you see at the kitchenware store. While some kitchen tools are essential, others lean toward the indulgent. (In other words, they're a lot of fun though hardly necessary.) It's certainly not essential to run out and purchase everything on these pages right away. You'll always find a way to make do with what you have at the moment. Improvising is part of the fun and challenge of cooking.

But as I tell everyone—whether they're just getting started with cooking or have been doing it for years—go out and buy an apron. You're going to be handling a lot of food and you have to have something to wipe your hands on when you can't find that darn towel. Here are the other kitchen tools that I count on regularly.

Knives

You want to know why some people don't like to cook? Because they've never held a high-quality knife in their hand. Once they experience the precision and strength of a sharp, durable blade, not only do they toss away their dull knives, but they look forward to working with their new knives every day. A cook must have quality cutlery for enjoyment, ease, and safety—cuts are more often a result of a dull knife not slicing the food properly than of a sharp knife.

An investment in superior knives is an investment in cooking itself. And when you're working with vegetables, where the standing order is always chop, chop, chop, your knives—good knives—are the most important kitchen tools you can own. High-carbon stainless steel blades and comfortable hard-rubber handles make the knife a powerful extension of your own hand.

- 2- to 3-inch paring knife: This short-blade knife is the perfect size for most peeling and slicing tasks. It also helps with garnishing duties.
- 4-inch serrated knife: With its serrated blade, this is ideal for cutting cleanly through tomatoes and other soft fruits and vegetables.

- 8-inch Japanese vegetable knife: This square-head blade is the workhorse of my knife collection. I use it every day for chopping, cutting, slicing, and mincing.
- 8-inch pointed chef's knife: Similar to the Japanese vegetable knife, this powerful blade is also designed for chopping, slicing, and cutting.
- 10-inch bread knife: Because of the long serrated blade, this knife makes quick and easy work of slicing through both doughy and crusty breads.

Get into the practice of running the sharp edge of your knives along a sharpening steel rod each time before you cook to keep the edges keen. Once a month I also use a sharpening stone to bring back an exceptionally sharp edge. Some stones require lubrication, and I find that water is better for thinner blades while a little vegetable oil works best for the bigger, heavier knives.

Wash and dry your knives after using them, and don't forget to store your knives in a safe place, separate from other small wares. Don't just throw them into a drawer with other utensils; the blades can be nicked that way. Use a wall-mounted magnetic strip (unless tall pets and kids are around) or a wooden knife holder for storage.

Cutting boards

There will probably always be a debate over which is the best material for cutting boards, wood or plastic. I think that as long as you clean your boards with soap and hot water after each use, there is nothing to worry about. But no matter which material you prefer, it's best to have more than one board. Big boards are essential for the large volume of vegetables you'll be working with. Since the aromas and flavors of different ingredients can linger on a cutting board, even after washing, you'll need a smaller board for stronger foods like garlic and onions. It's also nice to have a small plastic board for fruits and vegetables that might stain, like beets or strawberries.

Pots and pans

I insist on using heavy-bottomed pots and pans that conduct heat evenly, and you should too. The thickness of the material can be the difference between sautéing and burning. The manufacturing material can also affect that taste of foods. Whenever possible, use heavy-gauge stainless steel. It transfers heat evenly, won't warp over time, and doesn't give the food a tinny taste.

Pressure cooker

This appliance isn't just a time-saver, it's a great device for creating wonderful deep aromas and flavors, especially when cooking grains, root vegetables, and beans. A 4- or $5\frac{1}{2}$-quart-capacity pressure cooker has adequate space to make hearty stews, soups, and grain dishes.

Saucepans

Saucepans are ideal for so many tasks, from reheating soups to making sauces to boiling vegetables. Since this is such a useful type of pan, you should have at least two sizes with lids.

Sauté pan

Sauté pans are wide but shallow, and you can cook so many different foods in them. A 10-inch-diameter pan with a 3-quart capacity works very well for most jobs. Get one with a lid and a loop handle on the opposite side of the longer handle.

Frying pan

A frying pan, or skillet, has either high or low sides and is heavy so it stays put on the stove top. Having a cover means that you can use it for slow-cooking duties. Either a 10-inch or 12-inch-diameter frying pan will work just fine at home. Cast iron and stainless steel are preferred because of how evenly they conduct heat.

Stockpot

You will find these big pots ranging in capacity from 4 quarts to 20 quarts. A 10-quart pot should be big enough for most jobs. You certainly don't want to get one that's too small.

Baking pans

My thought about bakeware is the same as for pots and pans: Heavy, well-manufactured items are much more reliable. They last longer and cook the food more evenly.

Pie pans

Pie pans are found in 8-, 9-, and 10-inch diameters. Many dessert recipes call for a 9-inch pan, so start out with one or two of those. Ceramic and glass are good choices, allowing you to cut right in the pan.

Loaf pan

A rectangular Pyrex loaf pan allows you to see the bread—or whatever is inside—as it bakes. A good size pan to get is 9 inches by 5 inches by 2 inches deep.

Muffin pan

You'll find many sizes to fit your particular muffin fondness, from mini to giant.

Baking sheet

Measure the inside of your oven before purchasing a baking sheet, since there are several different sizes to choose from. Ideally, there should be about two inches of space separating the sheet from the oven sides.

Springform pan

The sides expand on this uniquely designed pan so that whatever is inside can be easily removed. You should have at least one 9-inch springform pan.

Small wares

Here is more kitchen stuff that I use regularly—most of which I'm sure you have already and some of which I'm sure you can do without.

Bamboo mats You might also see these called "sushi mats." They are made of bamboo sticks woven together with string and used to roll sheets of nori around rice and other sushi ingredients.

Blenders A large tabletop blender should have a stable base for pureeing soups, grinding nuts, making smoothies, and many other tasks without moving across the countertop. An immersion blender is essentially a mechanized handheld wand that can be lowered into nearly any size bowl. It's portable, but it's not nearly as powerful as a tabletop blender.

Bowls Bowls are as essential as they are basic. Stackable bowls for mixing and holding ingredients should range in size from the very small to the very large.

Cheesecloth Use unbleached cheesecloth to strain liquids and make bouquet garni—pouches of herbs used to flavor soups and sauces.

Citrus zester This cutting tool is pulled across the peel of citrus fruits to create highly aromatic strips.

Coffee mills Beyond its obvious use of grinding coffee beans, a mill does the same job for spices. Just don't use the same mill for both tasks.

Colander and strainer This wide bowl with holes in the bottom is used to rinse pasta, greens, fruits, and vegetables.

Cookie cutters The 3-inch rounds have many uses in the kitchen besides just making cookies.

Flame tamer A simple device that controls even a small flame, so that simmered dishes don't end up sticking to the bottom of the pan.

Food processor Used for both mixing and slicing ingredients quickly, food processors have become quite popular. If the capacity is at least 10 cups, it should handle most of your jobs.

Ice cream scoops 2- to 3-inch varieties can be used for scooping up cookie dough as well as making some entrée shapes.

Mandoline Paper-thin slices of vegetables can be made by moving the food across a mandoline. The board has blades affixed to its cutting surface, so julienne vegetables can be made quickly and safely. A V-slicer is a similar device creating the desired result.

Measuring cups and spoons Essential equipment for making exact measurements of liquids and dry ingredients. Get a 2- or 4-cup glass variety for liquids, and several cups of various sizes for dry ingredients. A set of measuring spoons should be sturdy and include sizes from $1/8$ teaspoon to 1 tablespoon.

Microplane grater With a high-quality stainless steel edge, this handheld tool is excellent for grating hard cheeses, citrus fruits, ginger, onions, and many other ingredients. The blade should be about $8^{1}/_{2}$ inches long, and make sure the handle feels good in your hand.

Mortar and pestle So primitive and yet so effective. These two pieces break down and grind the fibers of nuts, seeds, and spices to release a wondrous world of flavor and aroma. I love my Japanese version, called a *suribachi*. The inside of this earthenware mortar has ridges that facilitate grinding. The wooden pestle, called *surikogi*, won't wear down the ridges in the mortar. These versions are quite common in macrobiotic kitchens.

Parchment paper Always have a roll of this heavy paper on hand. It's used to line baking pans in place of a coating of fat. It resists moisture so foods won't stick.

Pastry brush You use this tool just like a paintbrush to apply oils, glazes, or other liquids to pastries, breads, and many other foods before or after cooking.

Pepper and spice mills These electric devices make quick work of grinding black pepper, white pepper, and myriad other spices to release more aromas and flavors. You can also use a coffee grinder as long as it's dedicated to spices.

Potato masher Using this simple handheld device makes quick work out of getting potatoes, parsnips, and other vegetables into their mashed form. Choose one with a comfortable handle.

Rice paddle There are wooden, stainless steel, and plastic versions of this large, flat-tipped spoon. It is the best tool for working with just-cooked rice dishes.

Rolling pin This is essential for rolling out smooth dough. Heavier pins seem to work best because they require less effort.

Salad spinner This kitchen tool removes excess moisture from greens, which means your salads will be crisp, not soggy.

Scale Not all recipes indicate the volume of ingredients. Some list ingredients by weight, so a scale proves very useful in those situations.

Skimmers A stainless steel fine-mesh giant spoon, called a "skimmer," is a must when deep-frying tempura or blanching vegetables or greens. The skimmer lifts the food from the pot, draining away the excess liquid, and the long handle helps your hand stay cool.

Spatulas, spoons, and ladles At least one of these extensions of your hand is used every single time you cook. So, if you're like me, you'll start picking up different sizes and shapes of them whenever you're out. Wood, hard rubber, and stainless steel all have their advantages in the right situation.

Spray bottle When a little bit of moisture is needed, a small spray bottle lets you be quick and accurate.

Steamer basket An 11-inch collapsible stainless steel steamer is great for uniformly steaming large batches of fresh vegetables. The 11-inch basket works in pans with 8- to 11-inch diameters.

Storage containers Like spoons, ladles, and spatulas, heavy plastic containers (with lids) can quickly become an obsession. But you will need a variety of sizes, so don't feel too guilty.

Stove-top smoker Made of stainless steel with a nonstick rack, this device allows you to smoke all types of foods and steam vegetables without using added fats.

Timer Because you might—okay, you *will*—be working on more than one task at once, a timer keeps you from losing track of what's going on around you. Some battery-operated models even have multiple settings.

Tongs Spring-loaded tongs are used for gripping and turning hot ingredients being roasted or grilled. There really isn't a good substitute for these, unless you have heat-resistant fingers.

Vegetable peeler A carbon-steel peeler that swivels to meet the contours of the vegetables is the best choice.

Vegetable strainer A fine-mesh strainer is used to capture smaller bits of chopped vegetables that might get through a colander when being rinsed.

Whisks You should have a large and a small whisk, both made of rust-free stainless steel. The different sizes will let you quickly combine ingredients no matter what size bowl you're working with.

The Basics of Working with Real Foods
Grains

Since ancient times, nutrient-rich whole grains cultivated from common grasses have been important foods for most cultures. However, in the modern era, grains are often heavily refined to remove the outer layer, or bran, so that they cook more quickly and are easier to chew. Unfortunately, the bran contains most of the fiber, B vitamins, and trace minerals. What is left after refining is devoid of many essential nutrients, so make sure you purchase whole grains or whole-grain products in order to get the most nutrition.

Here are some general guidelines for working with grains:

- It isn't necessary to soak grains before cooking. However, if you have the time or are using the grains medicinally, soaking them for 8 to 12 hours makes the nutrients more accessible to the body and the grain more digestible. Never cook with the soaking water.
- Whether soaking grains or not, always wash grains by placing them in a large pot or bowl. Cover with water and, using your hands, stir clockwise several times, then drain through a strainer. Repeat until the water comes out clean.
- The size of the grain determines the amount of water to be added and the cooking time.
- For large grains, such as brown rice and barley, 1 cup uncooked grain produces 2 cups cooked grain. When cooking, combine 1 cup grain and $1^1/_2$ cups water, then bring to a boil. Decrease the heat to a low simmer and cook, covered, for about 45 minutes. Yes, $1^1/_2$ cups water is less than the usual 2 cups, but trust me, it makes for drier and fluffier rice.
- For smaller grains, such as quinoa, millet, amaranth, polenta, and bulgur, 1 cup uncooked grain equals about $2^1/_2$ to 3 cups cooked grain. For cooking, bring $1^1/_2$ to 2 cups water to a boil. Add the grain and bring the water to a boil again; then decrease the heat to a low simmer and cook, covered, for about 25 to 40 minutes, depending on the size of the grain.
- Use a flame tamer between the pot and the fire to moderate the heat. This device prevents grains from sticking and burning on the bottom of the pot.
- Use $^1/_8$ to $^1/_4$ teaspoon sea salt to 1 cup water when cooking.

- In some recipes, toasting or sautéing grains before boiling is called for. This allows the grain to cook more quickly and yields a fluffier consistency. To pan-toast grains, heat a cast-iron skillet or a heavy frying pan over high heat until hot. Decrease the heat to medium-high, add the grains, and stir constantly with a wooden square-tipped spoon until the grain turns golden or darkens.
- Don't interrupt the cooking by lifting the lid.
- After cooking, use a rice paddle around the periphery of the cooked grains to allow the heat to escape. If the recipe calls for fluffing the grains, use a fork and be careful not to overdo it as the grains will start to clump together.
- Store cooked grains in airtight containers in the refrigerator for up to 3 days.
- To reheat, fork the grains apart and steam in steamer basket or lightly sauté with water or oil in a frying pan.
- Store uncooked grains in airtight containers in a cool, dry place. They can last for up to 9 months.

Dried beans and legumes

Dried beans, peas, and lentils are collectively called "legumes." Beans are high in complex carbohydrates, fiber, iron, and folic acid, and have more protein than any other vegetable food. Although the protein is incomplete (deficient in one or more essential amino acids), as long as you eat a complementary food, such as a grain or seed, in the same day, you'll get the benefits of a complete amino acid balance. We use a wide variety of beans in our recipes, including adzuki beans, black beans, pinto beans, and numerous white beans.

- Always rinse beans first, even if they come out of a package.
- 1 cup uncooked beans yields 2 to 3 cups cooked beans.
- Before cooking, if you have the time, it's best to soak beans for 8 to 12 hours with 1 part dried beans to 4 parts water. Soaking breaks down indigestible compounds, softens the skins, promotes faster cooking, and improves digestibility because the gas-causing enzymes in legumes are released into the

neutral. Regular table salt is stripped of its natural nutrients, then overloaded with additives to replace what was removed. But it still has no flavor.

On the other hand, sea salt that hasn't been refined is high in trace minerals and is loaded with flavor. Look for "whole" sea salt that comes in faintly gray crystals, granules, or fine powder. (The more popular brands are Lima, Celtic, Muramoto, or Si.) I prefer the finer-grain salt for most of my cooking and baking, although the coarser sea salt is good for salting water for pasta.

Gomasio This is the essential table condiment used in macrobiotic cuisine. It is made by blending toasted sesame seeds and sea salt. Its deep flavor replaces ordinary table salt. Gomasio is available in the spice aisle of some supermarkets and natural foods stores, but it's easy to make at home (see page 211).

Herbs You'll find the RFD recipes use fresh and dried herbs equally, and they can often be interchanged for each other. The general rule is two parts fresh to one part dry. Fresh herbs add a nice dimension to any dish and are wonderful to work with. The best way to keep them fresh is to place them in a glass or jar of water in the refrigerator. Gently cover them with plastic and they'll last up to 3 weeks. Change the water every few days.

Dried herbs are perfectly fine to use as well. You should always have your spice rack filled with many different varieties so you're never caught short when fresh herbs aren't available. They'll last up to a year if stored in a cool, dry place.

Spices In addition to dried herbs, keep your spice rack well stocked with spices. Dried spices will hold their potency for about a year when stored properly in a cool, dry place. One of the real joys of cooking is to buy whole spices and grind them yourself in a coffee grinder or by hand in a *suribachi* or with a mortar and pestle. The fresh aromas that are released and fill the kitchen are one of the many rewards of working with fresh spices.

Seitan

Seitan (SAY-tan), a versatile food used in quite a lot of vegetarian and vegan cuisine, is sometimes referred to as "wheat-meat" because of its chewy texture. It's made from the gluten (protein) in wheat flour. Seitan is best used in casseroles, stir-fries, and sandwiches, or just about anywhere you might previously have used meat. It can be oven-braised, baked, cooked in a pressure cooker, or deep-fried.

In the recipe section, I have given instructions on how to make two kinds of seitan (pages 175 and 189). Although it can be a bit time-consuming, I recommend making a weekly or bimonthly batch, storing it in the freezer, and using it as needed.

Vegetables

Central to Real Food Daily's recipes are vegetables. The vegetable kingdom is filled with an enormous range of colors, tastes, and textures. Each different subgroup contributes essential nutrients. I recommend always having some on hand from the following categories.

Green leafy This variety of vegetables is a source of vitamin C, calcium, and alkaline minerals. Most are quickly cooked or enjoyed raw. Common examples are kale, collard greens, bok choy, watercress, lettuces, and leeks. They should be kept in the crisper of the refrigerator.

Ground These plants grow near the ground and are less bitter than green leafy vegetables. They can be high in many vitamins and minerals, including the antioxidant beta-carotene. There are many to choose from, including cauliflower, broccoli, cabbage, green beans, snow peas, celery, cucumber, and summer and winter squash. They stay their freshest when stored in the refrigerator.

Root Grown underground, root vegetables are hearty-tasting foods that add strength to many dishes. Most are a good source of vitamins, minerals, and complex carbohydrates. Favorites include carrots, onions, radishes, turnips, parsnips, and rutabagas. Store them in a dry, dark area.

Baking flour

Good-tasting and better-for-you baked goods are a welcome part of any diet—in moderation, of course. As always, stay away from the heavily refined baking ingredients that have had their nutrition and flavor processed out. Stone-ground flour is preferable to steel-ground because the process retains more of the valuable enzymes and nutrients.

Whole wheat pastry flour is really the best choice for baking desserts. But because of the incredible demand for wheat-free desserts, at RFD we mostly use organic flours made from barley, oats, and rice. I think they match the feel and consistency of whole wheat flour the best. Organic unbleached white flour is also a suitable alternative for breads, cakes, and pastries.

Sweeteners

Refined white sugar is truly the epitome of the term "empty calorie." You won't find it in any of our recipes because it does nothing but turn food into junk food. There are much better sweetening alternatives that add better flavor.

Maple syrup is the primary sweetener we bake with. One hundred percent natural maple syrup is made by boiling and concentrating the sap from maple trees. Since it hasn't been refined, it brings a deep, rounded sweet flavor to baked goods. In some desserts, instead of the syrup we use dehydrated maple granules, called "maple crystals" or "maple sugar." They are twice as sweet as white sugar and much more flavorful.

We also use a variety of other sweeteners depending on the specific needs of the recipe: agave nectar, a mild sweetener extracted from the agave plant; barley malt, which is thick and has a maltlike flavor; and brown rice syrup, which is also thick, but mildly flavored.

Unusual real foods

You may not be quite as familiar with the following items, but each plays a unique role in Real Food Daily cuisine. Most can be found at specialty food markets and natural foods stores.

Agar This sea vegetable derivative is the vegan alternative to gelatin. Agar gels at room temperature, unlike conventional gelatin, which must be chilled. It's sold in long blocks, flakes, and powders. Agar will dissolve more easily if you first soak it for about 10 minutes in the liquid you are cooking it in.

Arrowroot A good replacement for cornstarch is this tasteless powder made from a tropical tuber that grows in the West Indies. It is used as a thickening agent to create a creamy texture. The key to working with arrowroot is to always dilute it in cold liquid before cooking.

Baking powder Commercial baking powders are made with aluminum sulfate, which can cause allergic reactions in some people. Make sure you purchase the aluminum-free type.

Baking soda This leavening agent is used to help baked goods rise and be tender. A combination of baking powder and baking soda can also act as a leavener and take the place of eggs.

Chocolate, nondairy Not all chocolate uses milk solids. Nondairy chocolate has a deep, rich flavor.

Coconut milk This fragrant, sweet liquid comes from combining fresh coconut meat and water and straining the liquid. When purchasing coconut milk from the Asian section of supermarkets, don't buy the sweetened variety.

Flaxseeds These small, flat brown seeds are often ground into flour and pressed into oil. They are also enjoyed in whole seed form.

Mirin This mildly sweet Japanese cooking wine is made from whole-grain rice. Its flavor rounds out acidic ingredients and goes especially well with soy sauce and sesame oil.

Nutritional yeast Not to be confused with brewer's yeast or active yeast, this product is a combination of inactive dry yeast and vitamins and is used as a seasoning. It has a nutty, cheeselike flavor.

Pickled ginger This culinary specialty is a mixture of sliced fresh gingerroot pickled with red shiso leaves and rice and umeboshi vinegars. Make sure you purchase only the pickled ginger found in a natural foods store, which contains no red dye, preservatives, or refined sugar.

Sea vegetables Sea vegetables have been around almost as long as the oceans have. They are marine algae and are classified by colors: red, brown, green, blue-green, and yellow-green. They contain up to twenty times the amount of minerals that land vegetables have. Seaweeds are widely available in Asian food markets and natural foods markets.

- Arame is a spaghetti-like dark brown sea vegetable rich in iron, calcium, and other minerals.
- Kombu is a wide, thick, dark green sea vegetable rich in vitamins and minerals.
- Nori is most commonly sold as thin black or dark purple sheets of dried sea vegetables. When roasted, nori turns green and can be used as the wrapper for sushi.

- Wakame is a long, thin, green sea vegetable with a sweet taste and delicate texture. It is high in protein, iron, and magnesium.

Shiitake mushrooms These flavorful fungi are prized as both a medicinal food and a culinary favorite of creative cooking. They are broad, dark brown mushrooms that grow in clusters either in the wild or cultivated on tree stumps. In Japan, they're considered a protein source in traditional cooking.

Shiso This aromatic leaf is related to mint and basil, with a flavor somewhere in between. Very popular in Japan, it is used to give flavoring and color to other foods.

Umeboshi This Japanese condiment is very salty and tart and popular at most Japanese meals, including breakfast. Made from pickled plums that are picked before they're ripe, then soaked in brine and red shiso leaves, umeboshi is available as whole plums, paste, and vinegar.

Vegan mayonnaise This egg- and dairy-free condiment is used just like regular mayonnaise.

Vinegars Using fruit- and grain-based vinegars is much more healthful because distilled vinegars are highly demineralizing.
- Brown rice vinegar is a light, amber-colored vinegar made from brown rice. It adds a mellow taste.
- Umeboshi vinegar is made from the umeboshi plum. It has a distinctive flavor that's a little salty and slightly fruity.

Wasabi This very pungent condiment (available in either paste or powder form) is made from the root of an Asian plant. Wasabi is often referred to as "Japanese horseradish."

Worcestershire sauce Vegan versions of this savory condiment don't include anchovies.

The top twenty real foods to always have in your kitchen

- Brown rice
- Ginger
- Maple syrup or maple crystals
- Mirin
- Miso
- Nuts and seeds
- Oats
- Olive oil
- Pasta
- Quinoa
- Sea salt
- Soymilk
- Tahini
- Tamari
- Tempeh
- Tofu
- Umeboshi
- Vegetables, green leafy
- Vegetables, ground
- Vegetables, root

Recipes

Starters and small plates

Hummus with pita

Always a sure bet at any get-together, no matter how big or small, hummus is traditionally served with pita bread but can also be used as a dip or spread with crudités and crackers. Be sure to allow the garbanzos to cool completely after they cook so the heat from the beans doesn't "cook" the garlic and other seasonings and change the fresh flavors that are so wonderful in this hummus. Cooking the garbanzo beans in a pressure cooker rather than in a regular pot cuts their cooking time by more than half. If you don't have a pressure cooker, just cook the beans in a regular pot for 2 to 3 hours, adding more hot water as needed, until they're tender. You can substitute 3 1/2 cups of canned garbanzo beans for the dried garbanzo beans.

Place the beans and kombu in a large bowl. Add enough cold water to cover the beans by 3 inches. Let stand overnight. Drain and rinse the beans, reserving the kombu.

Combine the beans, the kombu, and the 8 cups of water in a 4 1/4-quart pressure cooker. Lock the lid into place. Bring the pressure to high over high heat. Decrease the heat to low and cook for 40 minutes. Remove from the heat and let stand until the pressure reduces, about 15 minutes. Carefully remove the lid. Drain, reserving about 1/3 cup of the cooking liquid. Discard the kombu and cool the beans completely.

Combine the cooked beans, tahini, lemon juice, olive oil, and garlic in a food processor. Blend until smooth, adding enough reserved cooking liquid to form a creamy consistency. Blend in the salt, black pepper, and cayenne pepper.

Transfer the hummus to a wide, shallow serving bowl. Serve with the pita wedges, cucumber slices, and tomato wedges.

The hummus will keep for 2 days, covered and refrigerated.

1 1/2	cups dried garbanzo beans
1	(2- to 3-inch) piece kombu
8	cups water
1/3	cup roasted tahini
1/2	cup freshly squeezed lemon juice (about 3 lemons)
3	tablespoons extra-virgin olive oil
1	teaspoon minced garlic
1 1/2	teaspoons sea salt
1/4	teaspoon freshly ground black pepper
1/8	teaspoon cayenne pepper
4	whole wheat pita breads, cut into wedges
1/2	cucumber, unpeeled, thinly sliced diagonally
1	tomato, cut into wedges

cashew cheddar cheese

This cheese is great for shredding or melting. Cashews work better than other nuts because they blend into such a creamy, rich consistency. If you're not satisfied with the cheese's final consistency or texture, blame the agar flakes; all store-bought brands of agar flakes are cut differently, which unfortunately affects the amount added if measured by volume. If you'd rather not learn the hard way as I did, go by the provided weight rather than cup measure.

1 1/4 cups raw cashews

1/2 cup nutritional yeast

2 teaspoons onion powder

2 teaspoons sea salt

1 teaspoon garlic powder

1/8 teaspoon ground white pepper

3 1/2 cups unsweetened plain soymilk

1 cup agar flakes (about 2 ounces)

1/2 cup canola oil

1/4 cup yellow miso

2 tablespoons freshly squeezed lemon juice (about 1 lemon)

Using the pulse button, finely grind the cashews in a food processor; don't allow the cashews to turn into a paste. Add the nutritional yeast, onion powder, salt, garlic powder, and white pepper. Pulse three more times to blend in the spices.

Combine the soymilk, agar, and oil in a heavy saucepan. Bring to a simmer over high heat. Decrease the heat to medium-low, cover, and simmer, stirring occasionally, for 10 minutes, or until the agar is dissolved. With the food processor running, gradually pour the soymilk mixture through the feed tube and into the cashew mixture. Blend for 2 minutes, or until very smooth and creamy, and then blend in the miso and lemon juice.

For grated or sliced cheese, transfer the cheese to a container, cover, and refrigerate about 4 hours, until very firm. Once it's firm, grate or slice the cheese as desired.

For melted cheese, use the cheese immediately as melted cheese. Alternatively, make the cheese in advance, cover, and refrigerate. When you're ready to use the cheese, melt it in a saucepan over medium heat until smooth and creamy, stirring frequently. If needed, add more soymilk for a thinner consistency.

For Jalapeño Cashew Cheddar Cheese: Stir 2 tablespoons of minced jalapeño chiles into 2 cups of melted cheese.

The cheese will keep for 4 days, covered and refrigerated.

Spring rolls with raw mango sauce

Eating these spring rolls is an excellent way to get your daily vegetables. Rice paper, used often in Vietnamese cooking, comes in edible round, translucent sheets made not from rice, but from *Tetrapanax papyrifer,* a shrubby tree often referred to as the rice-paper plant. To make this dish strictly raw, use butter lettuce leaves instead of the rice paper as a wrap.

5 cups hot water

8 (9-inch-diameter) rice paper sheets

1¼ cups very thinly sliced napa cabbage

1 cup very thinly sliced red cabbage

⅔ cup julienned green onions (white and green parts)

⅔ cup julienned peeled carrots

⅔ cup julienned peeled daikon radish

⅔ cup julienned red bell pepper

⅓ cup chopped raw peanuts or almonds (optional)

½ cup lightly packed fresh cilantro leaves

8 large fresh mint leaves

1¼ cups Raw Mango Sauce (recipe follows)

Pour 5 cups of hot water into a large bowl. Using tongs, dip 1 rice paper sheet in the water for 7 seconds. Remove from the water and place the rice paper on a clean, moist towel. Let stand for 2 minutes (if the rice paper isn't pliable, moisten it with more water).

Place one-eighth of the napa cabbage and red cabbage across the center of the rice paper. Top with one-eighth each of the green onions, carrots, radish, and red bell pepper. Sprinkle 2 teaspoons of peanuts over the vegetables. Top with a few cilantro leaves and 1 mint leaf. Fold the sides of the rice paper over the ends of the filling. Starting at 1 long side, roll tightly into a cylinder. Place the spring roll on a platter and cover with plastic wrap. Repeat with the remaining rice paper sheets, vegetables, peanuts, and herbs.

Cut each spring roll diagonally in half and arrange them on the platter. Serve the sauce alongside.

The spring rolls will keep for 8 hours, covered and refrigerated.

raw mango sauce

I love this cool and refreshing sauce, especially on just a simple mixed greens salad. My kids eat it with the Seitan Fingers (page 48). Be sure to strain this sauce after it's pureed. It may look velvety smooth, but once you strain it, you'll notice the mango's thin fibrous strands left behind, which lend an undesirable texture.

Soak the dates in a bowl of water for 2 hours. Drain and transfer to a blender. Add the mango, onion, lemon juice, orange juice, nama shoyu, garlic, ginger, and jalapeño chile. Blend until the sauce is smooth. Strain the sauce into a serving bowl. Serve at room temperature or cover and refrigerate until cold.

The sauce will keep for 2 days, covered and refrigerated.

6 pitted dates

3/4 cup coarsely chopped pitted peeled mango (about 1 mango)

1/4 cup chopped onion

1/4 cup freshly squeezed lemon juice (about 2 lemons)

1/4 cup freshly squeezed orange juice (about 1 orange)

1 1/2 tablespoons nama shoyu

1 clove garlic

1/2 teaspoon minced peeled fresh ginger

1/4 teaspoon minced jalapeño chile

LIVING FOODS

Raw foods are sometimes called "living foods" because they contain active enzymes that are considered to be the life force of the food. People who eat mostly living foods believe these enzymes greatly benefit the body, and that cooking fruits, vegetables, legumes, nuts, and seeds above 118°F destroys the enzymes.

As with any other nutrition strategy, there are many opinions on the effectiveness of eating a diet that mostly consists of raw fruits and vegetables. The opposing opinion is that heat activates the enzymes and food needs to be cooked in order for your body to assimilate most of the nutrients. The reality is that science has not conclusively proved either side's arguments.

What's not in dispute is that living food can taste wonderful, and that there is certainly nothing wrong with eating a lot of fresh fruits and vegetables every day. While most people might think the only raw food options are salads, juices, and fruit from the tree, in the last few years living food has been elevated to a high-art cuisine, with several raw food cookbooks being published and many new restaurants opening that serve exclusively living foods.

At Real Food Daily we offer some living food dishes, because they're healthful, yes, but mostly because they taste delicious. For some of the recipes in this book, raw ingredients can be substituted for cooked. For example, raw tahini and nama shoyu can be used instead of roasted tahini and tamari; and our Raw Cashew Cheese (page 47) works well in some of the recipes that call for our house-made tofu cheeses.

Living paradise with raw tomato sauce

A spiral slicer is a handy little tool to have around. Used often in Japanese cuisine, it cuts vegetables (such as the daikon radish in this recipe) into spaghetti-like strands and other fancy and delicate shapes. It can be found at most Japanese markets and some specialty cookware stores. If you don't have a spiral slicer, cut the daikon radish into thin julienne strips.

1/2 cup Raw Cashew Cheese (opposite page)

1 (4-inch) piece daikon radish, peeled

5 cups hot water

8 (9-inch-diameter) rice paper sheets

2 cups fresh arugula (about 1 ounce)

1 cup unpeeled, julienned English cucumber

3/4 cup julienned yellow squash

2/3 cup julienned red bell pepper

1/2 cup julienned green onions (white and green parts)

1/2 cup julienned peeled carrot

1/2 cup julienned zucchini

1 1/2 cups Raw Tomato Sauce (recipe follows)

Fill a small resealable plastic bag with the cheese. Using scissors, snip one corner of the bag to allow the cheese to be squeezed out. Refrigerate until ready to use.

Using a spiral vegetable slicer, cut the daikon into long, curly, thin strands resembling spaghetti. Set aside.

Pour 5 cups of hot water into a large bowl. Using tongs, dip 1 rice paper sheet in the water for 7 seconds. Remove from the water and place the rice paper on a clean, moist towel. Let stand for 2 minutes (if the rice paper isn't pliable, moisten it with more water).

Place one-eighth of the arugula across the center of the rice paper. Top with one-eighth each of the radish, cucumber, yellow squash, red bell pepper, green onions, carrot, and zucchini. Pipe the cheese over the vegetables.

Fold the sides of the rice paper over the ends of the filling. Starting at 1 long side, roll tightly into a cylinder. Place the spring roll on a platter and cover with plastic wrap. Repeat with the remaining rice paper sheets, vegetables, and cheese. Serve with the sauce alongside.

The spring rolls will keep for 8 hours, covered and refrigerated.

raw tomato sauce

Raw sun-dried tomatoes add a depth of flavor and richness that would normally occur only in a cooked sauce. Soaking the tomatoes in the blender and then adding all the remaining ingredients eliminates an extra bowl to clean up. Extra-virgin olive oil is used in this raw sauce not only for the wonderful flavor it imparts, but also because it's cold-pressed and never heated above 118°F.

1/2 cup sun-dried tomatoes (not packed in oil)

1 cup water

2 plum tomatoes, quartered

1/4 cup coarsely chopped onion

1/4 cup lightly packed fresh basil leaves

2 tablespoons extra-virgin olive oil

3 cloves garlic

3/4 teaspoon sea salt

1/4 teaspoon freshly ground black pepper

1/8 teaspoon crushed red pepper flakes

Place the sun-dried tomatoes in a blender. Add the water and soak for 2 hours, or until softened. Add the plum tomatoes, onion, basil, olive oil, garlic, salt, black pepper, and red pepper. Blend until smooth. Transfer to a bowl and serve at room temperature.

The sauce will keep for 2 days, covered and refrigerated. Bring the sauce to room temperature before using.

RAW CASHEW CHEESE

Soaking nuts not only makes them softer and easier to blend, it also makes them easier to digest, especially when they remain uncooked, as in this cheese. It's essential to plan ahead and allow the cheese to set up for at least a day.

Makes about 1 1/4 cups

1 1/2 cups raw cashews

1/3 cup water

2 teaspoons freshly squeezed lemon juice

2 cloves garlic

1/2 teaspoon sea salt

Place the cashews in a bowl and add enough cold water to cover by 2 inches. Soak for 2 hours, and then drain.

Combine the cashews, 1/3 cup water, lemon juice, garlic, and salt in a food processor and blend, scraping down the sides of the bowl occasionally, for 5 minutes, or until very smooth.

Transfer the cheese to a small bowl. Cover and let stand at room temperature at least 1 day and up to 2 days. Refrigerate the cheese until ready to use. The cheese will keep for up to 5 days, covered and refrigerated.

Seitan fingers with tamarind sauce

Kids love this dish because of the size and shape and the crisp coating provided by the bread crumbs. These taste just as good with ketchup as with the Tamarind Sauce. Be sure to refrigerate the coated seitan at least 1 hour before frying. This will help the coating better adhere to the seitan during frying.

$^1/_2$ cup whole wheat pastry flour

$^3/_4$ teaspoon arrowroot

$^1/_4$ teaspoon ground ginger

$^1/_4$ teaspoon sea salt

$^1/_8$ teaspoon freshly ground black pepper

Pinch of baking powder

$^1/_2$ cup unsweetened plain soymilk

12 ounces Chicken-Style Seitan (page 175)

$1^1/_2$ cups bread crumbs

Canola oil, for frying

$2^1/_3$ cups Tamarind Sauce (recipe follows)

Whisk the flour, arrowroot, ginger, salt, pepper, and baking powder in a large bowl to blend. Whisk in the soymilk to form a smooth, thin batter.

Cut the seitan dough into eighteen 4 by $^1/_2$ by $^1/_2$-inch strips. Dip the seitan strips in the batter to coat completely, then dip into the bread crumbs to coat (you'll have some batter left over). Place the coated seitan strips on a baking sheet. Cover and refrigerate at least 1 hour and up to 1 day.

Heat 1 inch of oil in a large, heavy frying pan over medium-high heat. When the oil is hot, add the coated seitan strips and fry for $1^1/_2$ minutes per side, or until heated through, crisp, and golden brown. Using a metal spatula or tongs, transfer the seitan to a paper towel–lined plate to drain.

Arrange the seitan strips on a platter and serve immediately with Tamarind Sauce.

tamarind sauce

Tamarinds are also known as Indian dates. In this recipe, the tart flavor of tamarind combines with the sweet dates and raisins to create a delicious sweet-and-sour sauce. You can find tamarind pulp at most East Indian shops and some Mexican and Asian markets.

2¾ cups (or more) water

1 pound tamarind pulp

2 teaspoons canola oil

½ cup chopped onion

1 tablespoon minced peeled fresh ginger

1 tablespoon minced jalapeño chile

½ teaspoon garam masala

½ cup pitted dates

½ cup raisins

1 teaspoon sea salt

Bring 2 cups of the water to a boil in a heavy saucepan. Remove from the heat, add the tamarind, and stir until the tamarind pulp dissolves. Strain the mixture into a bowl, pressing on the solids to extract as much pulp and liquid as possible. Discard the seeds and solids and set the tamarind mixture aside.

Heat the oil in a heavy saucepan over medium heat. Add the onion and sauté for 3 minutes, or until tender. Add the ginger and jalapeño chile, and sauté for 1 minute, or until fragrant. Stir in the garam masala, then the dates, raisins, salt, and the remaining ¾ cup water. Cover and simmer for 12 minutes, or until the dried fruit is tender and the liquid is completely absorbed. Stir into the tamarind mixture.

Working in batches, transfer the tamarind mixture to a blender and blend until smooth. Strain the sauce into a bowl, adding more water if you prefer a thinner consistency. Serve the sauce warm or at room temperature.

The sauce will keep for 2 days, covered and refrigerated.

Green noodle roll

This is a fun dish and great party food because of the green mugwort soba noodles (although regular soba noodles or sushi rice would work well, too). Mugwort, a wild herb, has a unique flavor and a mild lime green color. Japanese cucumbers resemble English cucumbers but are smaller and more slender. Shiso leaves, a member of the basil and mint family, lend a wonderful flavor. Shiso leaves and Japanese cucumbers may be found at Japanese markets.

4 ounces mugwort soba noodles or regular soba noodles

1 teaspoon sea salt

Marinated Shiitake Mushrooms

$1/2$ cup water

3 tablespoons mirin

2 tablespoons tamari

1 teaspoon minced peeled fresh ginger

8 dried shiitake mushrooms

2 tablespoons toasted sesame oil

1 teaspoon minced garlic

4 nori sheets

4 teaspoon toasted sesame seeds (see page 41)

8 shiso leaves

2 slices Grilled Herb Tofu (page 33), cut into $1/4$-inch-wide strips

2 green onions (white and green parts), cut lengthwise into $1/8$-inch-wide strips

$1/2$ Japanese cucumber, peeled, seeded, and cut lengthwise into $1/4$-inch-wide strips

$1/2$ firm but ripe avocado, peeled, pitted, and cut into 8 thin wedges

$1/4$ cup thinly sliced pickled ginger

Lemon-Ginger Dipping Sauce (see page 53), for dipping

Bring a large pot of water to a boil. Add the noodles and salt. Boil, stirring often, for 8 minutes, or until the noodles are tender but still firm to the bite. Drain, then rinse the noodles under cold water to cool completely. Drain well and pat dry.

To make the marinated mushrooms: Whisk the $1/2$ cup water, mirin, tamari, and ginger in a bowl. Add the mushrooms and soak for 30 minutes, and then stir in the sesame oil and garlic. Heat a heavy skillet over medium-low heat. Add the mushroom mixture and simmer gently, turning the mushrooms once, for 15 minutes, or until the mushrooms are tender and the liquid evaporates. Cool completely, and then cut the mushrooms into $1/4$-inch-wide strips.

To assemble the roll: Place 1 nori sheet, shiny side down, on a bamboo mat with 1 long side positioned closest to you. Arrange 1 cup of the noodles loosely and evenly over the nori sheet, leaving a $1/2$-inch border on the top long side. Sprinkle with 1 teaspoon of the sesame seeds. Lay 2 of the shiso leaves side by side atop the noodles at the long side closest to you. Arrange one-fourth of the mushrooms, tofu, green onions, cucumber, and avocado horizontally across the middle of the shiso leaves. Lay the one-fourth of the ginger slices over the

(continued)

Butternut squash, corn, and cilantro phyllo rolls

You could almost call these pastries: They're delicate, sweet, and flaky, with a slight crunch provided by the corn. Canola oil replaces the melted butter traditionally used with phyllo and helps crisp the rolls as they bake.

Heat the olive oil in a large, heavy frying pan over medium heat. Add the onions, celery, and garlic and sauté for 5 minutes, or until the onions are translucent. Add the squash and carrots, and sauté 25 minutes longer, or until the squash and carrots are crisp-tender. Add the cabbage and corn, and sauté for 4 minutes, or until the cabbage wilts and the liquid evaporates (the mixture should be thick and chunky at this point). Stir in the cilantro and salt. Cool to room temperature and stir in the cheese.

Preheat the oven to 375°F. Line a large, heavy baking sheet with parchment paper. Unroll the phyllo sheets on a dry flat surface. Carefully remove 1 phyllo sheet and lay it on a work surface (keep the remaining phyllo covered with plastic wrap and a damp kitchen towel). Brush the phyllo sheet with some of the canola oil. Cut the phyllo sheet crosswise into three 4-inch-wide strips. Place 2 generous tablespoons of the butternut squash mixture on 1 short end of each phyllo strip. Working with 1 phyllo strip at a time, roll up the phyllo to enclose the squash mixture, folding in the sides as for a burrito, and brushing the edge with more oil to seal. Transfer the rolls to the prepared baking sheet, seam side down, and brush the tops with more oil. Repeat with the remaining phyllo sheets, oil, and butternut squash mixture, forming 24 rolls total.

Bake for 25 minutes, or until golden brown. Cool slightly, then arrange the rolls on a platter and serve warm.

Stored in an airtight container, the uncooked rolls will keep for 1 week in the freezer. To bake, place the frozen rolls on a baking sheet (do not thaw them) and bake for 35 minutes, or until golden brown.

2   tablespoons olive oil

2   cups finely chopped onions

1/2   cup finely chopped celery

2   teaspoons minced garlic

1 3/4   pounds butternut squash, peeled, seeded, and cut into 1/4-inch cubes

1   cup julienned peeled carrots

1   cup very thinly sliced green cabbage

1   cup yellow corn kernels (about 2 ears of corn)

1/4   cup finely chopped fresh cilantro

1/4   teaspoon sea salt

3/4   cup Tofu Ricotta Cheese (page 157)

8   frozen whole wheat phyllo pastry sheets, thawed

1/2   cup canola oil

Sea vegetable and cucumber phyllo purses

This recipe will make anyone a fan of sea vegetables. Wakame is a mild-tasting sea vegetable that provides chlorophyll, enzymes, beta-carotene, and B vitamins. It's available at Japanese markets and in the Asian section of natural foods stores.

3/4 ounce dried wakame

3 cucumbers, peeled, halved lengthwise, seeded, and cut into paper-thin slices

1 1/2 teaspoons sea salt

2 tablespoons olive oil

1 1/4 cups finely chopped onion

3 tablespoons freshly squeezed lemon juice (about 1 lemon)

4 teaspoons white or yellow miso

3 tablespoons roasted tahini

3 tablespoons finely chopped fresh parsley

1 1/2 teaspoons finely grated lemon zest

1 1/2 teaspoons hot pepper sauce

6 frozen whole wheat phyllo pastry sheets, thawed

1/2 cup (about) canola oil

Place the wakame in a bowl and add enough cold water to cover by 1 inch. Let stand for 20 minutes, or until tender. Drain well and pat dry. Cut away and discard the center rib. Cut the wakame leaves into 1-inch squares, and then place them in a bowl.

Meanwhile, toss the cucumbers and 3/4 teaspoon of the salt in a large bowl. Let stand for 15 minutes, tossing occasionally. Squeeze the cucumbers to extract as much liquid as possible. Pat the cucumber slices with paper towels, then add to the wakame.

Heat the olive oil in a heavy skillet over medium heat. Add the onion and sauté for 5 minutes, or until golden brown. Cool to room temperature.

Whisk the lemon juice and miso in a large bowl to blend. Whisk in the tahini, parsley, zest, hot pepper sauce, and the remaining 3/4 teaspoon salt. Stir in the wakame mixture and the sautéed onions.

Preheat the oven to 375°F. Line a large, heavy baking sheet with parchment paper. Unroll the phyllo sheets on a dry flat surface. Carefully remove 1 phyllo sheet and lay it on a work surface (keep the remaining phyllo covered with plastic wrap and a damp kitchen towel). Brush the phyllo sheet with some of the canola oil. Top with a second phyllo sheet, and brush it with oil. Repeat with a third phyllo sheet and oil. Cut the layered sheets into twelve 4-inch squares. Place 1 generous tablespoon of the wakame mixture in the center of each layered phyllo square. Working with 1 layered phyllo square at a time, bring the corners and sides of the pastry together over the filling and twist to enclose the filling completely, forming a purse. Transfer the purses to the prepared baking sheet and brush the tops with more oil. Repeat with the remaining phyllo sheets, oil, and wakame mixture, forming 24 purses total.

Bake for 25 minutes, or until golden brown. Cool slightly, then arrange the purses on a platter and serve warm.

Stored in an airtight container, the uncooked purses will keep for 1 week in the freezer. When you're ready to bake them, place the frozen purses on a baking sheet (do not thaw them) and bake for 35 minutes, or until golden brown.

Salsas, sauces, and gravies

Hickory barbecue sauce

A stove-top smoker, a wonderful tool that lends a natural smoky flavor to many different foods, is used here to smoke the tomatoes and add a terrific dimension of flavor to the sauce. If you don't have a stove-top smoker, you can omit the plum tomatoes and replace the canned tomatoes with a 28-ounce can of whole tomatoes. Although you won't get the smoky flavor, the sauce will still be delicious.

Prepare a stove-top smoker according to the manufacturer's instructions. Smoke the tomatoes over medium heat for 30 minutes, or until the skins loosen and the tomatoes soften.

Meanwhile, heat the olive oil in a large, heavy saucepan over medium heat. Add the onion and sauté for 8 minutes, or until translucent. Stir in the garlic and mango and sauté for 8 minutes, or until the mango is mushy. Add the smoked tomatoes, canned tomatoes with their juices, water, tomato paste, maple syrup, molasses, vinegar, lemon juice, Worcestershire sauce, salt, pepper, mustard powder, onion powder, and garlic powder. Bring to a boil over medium-high heat. Decrease the heat to medium-low and simmer, uncovered, stirring occasionally, for 30 minutes, or until the sauce thickens slightly and the tomatoes are very tender. Cool slightly.

Using a handheld immersion blender, puree the sauce until smooth. Alternatively, working in batches, puree in a regular blender until smooth.

The sauce will keep for 3 days, covered and refrigerated.

4 plum tomatoes
1 tablespoon olive oil
1 onion, chopped
4 cloves garlic, finely chopped
1 mango, peeled, pitted, and chopped
1 (15-ounce) can whole tomatoes
1 cup water
1 (6-ounce) can tomato paste
3/4 cup maple syrup
1/2 cup light unsulfured molasses
1/4 cup apple cider vinegar
2 tablespoons freshly squeezed lemon juice (about 1 lemon)
2 tablespoons vegan Worcestershire sauce
1 1/2 teaspoons sea salt
1 teaspoon freshly ground black pepper
1 teaspoon mustard powder
1 teaspoon onion powder
1/2 teaspoon garlic powder

Teriyaki sauce

This fruity teriyaki sauce is used on the Grilled Seitan with Sweet Rice and Pineapple (page 169) and will take any grilled or broiled seitan, tempeh, or tofu dish to another dimension.

³/₄ cup water

³/₄ cup maple syrup

²/₃ cup chopped cored peeled pineapple (about ¹/₄ pineapple)

²/₃ cup chopped pitted peeled mango (about 1 mango)

²/₃ cup freshly squeezed orange juice (about 2 oranges)

¹/₂ cup mirin

¹/₂ cup tamari

3 tablespoon minced peeled fresh ginger

2 tablespoons toasted sesame oil

1 tablespoon minced garlic

Combine all the ingredients in a large, heavy saucepan and bring to a simmer over high heat. Decrease the heat to medium and simmer uncovered for 15 minutes, or until the fruit is very tender.

Using a handheld immersion blender or a regular blender, puree the sauce until completely smooth. Strain through a fine-mesh strainer and discard any solids.

The sauce will keep up to 3 days, covered and refrigerated. Rewarm before using.

Basil pesto

Toasting the pine nuts is a key step to making this pesto, as it lends a rich and nutty flavor. Use this pesto in the Cold Penne Salad (page 113) or with your favorite pasta, or stir in a little vegan mayonnaise and use it as a sandwich spread.

Blend all the ingredients in a food processor until smooth and creamy. The pesto will keep for 2 days, covered and refrigerated.

2 cups packed fresh basil leaves

$1/2$ cup pine nuts, toasted (see page 41)

$1/4$ cup extra-virgin olive oil

8 cloves garlic

3 tablespoons yellow miso

1 teaspoon freshly ground black pepper

Guacamole

RFD guacamole is so rich and sinful tasting that people never believe we make it without sour cream. Using ripe avocados makes all the difference, so look for avocados that are firm but yield slightly when pressed.

Toss the tomato, onion, cilantro, lemon juice, and salt in a bowl. Let stand for 20 minutes. Mash the avocados in a large bowl. Stir in the tomato mixture and season to taste with more salt, if desired.

Transfer to a serving bowl and serve.

The guacamole will keep for 4 hours, covered tightly and refrigerated. Stir before serving.

1 tomato, diced

$1/2$ small white onion, finely diced

$1/2$ cup chopped fresh cilantro

3 tablespoons freshly squeezed lemon juice (about 1 lemon)

$1 1/4$ teaspoons sea salt

4 ripe avocados, peeled, pitted, and coarsely chopped

Soups

Butternut squash soup

Serve this soup as a delicious first course for any traditional winter holiday dinner. I use a heavy-duty peeler to cut through the tough skin of butternut squash and a microplane grater to remove the orange zest from the oranges.

Heat the oil in a heavy stockpot over medium-high heat. Add the onions, celery, garlic, and ginger and sauté for 5 minutes, or until the vegetables are tender. Stir in the stock and squash, cover, and bring to a simmer over high heat. Decrease the heat to medium-low and simmer, stirring occasionally, for 30 minutes, or until the squash is tender. Stir in the maple syrup, tamari, orange zest, salt, pepper, and nutmeg.

Using a handheld immersion blender, puree the soup in the pot until smooth. Alternatively, working in batches, puree in a regular blender until smooth. Stir in the soymilk.

Ladle the soup into individual bowls. Sprinkle with additional nutmeg and serve.

The soup will keep for 2 days, covered and refrigerated.

1	tablespoon canola oil
2	onions, chopped
3	stalks celery, chopped
3	cloves garlic, chopped
1	(1-inch) piece fresh ginger, peeled and finely chopped
8	cups vegetable stock (page 77) or water
2¾	pounds butternut squash, peeled, seeded, and cubed
¼	cup maple syrup
2	tablespoons tamari
2	teaspoons finely grated orange zest
1	teaspoon sea salt
½	teaspoon freshly ground black pepper
¼	teaspoon ground nutmeg, plus more for garnish
1	cup plain soymilk

Asparagus and cilantro soup

When asparagus is in season you simply must make this soup. The rather exotic, bitter-tasting asparagus pairs amazingly well with the fresh, clean flavor of cilantro.

1   tablespoon olive oil

1   large onion, coarsely
     chopped

3   stalks celery, coarsely
     chopped

3   cloves garlic, chopped

1   small russet potato,
     peeled and coarsely
     chopped

1   tablespoon chopped
     fresh basil

2   teaspoons chopped
     fresh oregano

1   teaspoon ground cumin

6   cups vegetable stock
     (page 77) or water

2   pounds asparagus,
     trimmed, tips reserved,
     and stalks cut crosswise
     into 1-inch pieces

1   tablespoon tamari

2   teaspoons sea salt

1/8 teaspoon freshly
     ground white pepper

1/2 cup finely chopped
     fresh cilantro

Heat the olive oil in a heavy stockpot over medium heat. Add the onion, celery, and garlic, and sauté for 8 minutes, or until the onion is translucent. Stir in the potato, basil, oregano, and cumin. Add the stock and bring to a simmer over high heat. Decrease the heat to medium-low, cover, and simmer, stirring occasionally, for 10 minutes, or until the potato is almost tender. Add the asparagus stalks and simmer for 5 minutes, or until the asparagus is tender and the potato is very tender.

Using a handheld immersion blender, puree the soup in the pot until smooth. Alternatively, working in batches, puree in a regular blender until smooth. Stir in the tamari, salt, and white pepper. Return the soup to a simmer, then stir in the cilantro.

Meanwhile, cook the reserved asparagus tips in a saucepan of boiling water for 1 minute, or until crisp-tender. Drain, then cut the asparagus tips in half lengthwise.

Ladle the soup into individual bowls. Garnish with the asparagus tips and serve.

The soup and uncooked asparagus tips will keep for 2 days, covered separately and refrigerated.

Country-style miso soup

Usually miso soup is brothy with just a garnish of vegetables. This heartier country-style version is made with lots of vegetables. Use broad wakame leaves (sometimes labeled as "wild Atlantic wakame") rather than the thinly shredded variety. You can find them at Japanese markets and in the Asian foods section at most natural foods stores. Mild white or pale yellow miso won't be as overpowering in this soup as the stronger-tasting red or brown miso would be.

Combine 5 cups of the water and the mushrooms in a bowl. Combine the remaining 5 cups water and the wakame in another bowl. Let each stand for 1 hour, or until each is tender. Using a slotted spoon, transfer the mushrooms to a work surface and thinly slice them. Using the slotted spoon, transfer the wakame to the work surface. Cut away and discard the center veins, then cut the leaves into bite-size squares.

Using a coffee filter or lining a sieve with several layers of cheesecloth, strain the mushroom and wakame soaking liquids into a heavy stockpot. Add the mushrooms, wakame, cabbage, radish, celery, carrots, and onion. Cover and bring to a simmer over high heat. Decrease the heat to medium-low and simmer, stirring occasionally, for 20 minutes, or until the vegetables are very tender. Remove from the heat.

Prepared up to this point, the soup will keep for 1 day, covered and refrigerated. Before continuing, bring the soup to a simmer over medium-high heat, stirring occasionally.

Just before serving, rest a sieve atop the pot of hot soup, submerging the bottom of the sieve into the soup. Stir the miso in the sieve, dissolving it into the soup. Stir the soup to fully blend in the miso. Don't allow the soup to boil vigorously once the miso has been added, since doing so destroys some of the nutrients in the miso.

Ladle the soup into individual bowls. Sprinkle with the green onions and serve.

10 cups water

4 dried shiitake mushrooms

$1/2$ ounce wakame leaves

$1/4$ head napa cabbage, cut crosswise into $1/2$-inch-thick strips

1 (5-inch) piece daikon radish, peeled, halved lengthwise, and cut crosswise into $1/4$-inch-thick slices

4 stalks celery, cut crosswise into $1/4$-inch-thick slices

4 large carrots, peeled, halved lengthwise, and cut crosswise into $1/4$-inch-thick slices

1 small onion, halved and cut crosswise into $1/4$-inch-thick slices

$1 1/4$ cups white or yellow miso

3 green onions (white and green parts), thinly sliced diagonally

Cream of napa cabbage and watercress soup with basil

This is a very easy soup to make since most of the ingredients are simply combined in a pot and simmered. The oats not only add nutritional value, they also give the soup a fuller, silky texture. Swirl some Red Pepper Crème (page 85) over the soup, if desired. The contrasting colors make a dramatic presentation, and the flavor of the crème pairs deliciously with the basil. This is also great served chilled in the hotter months.

5   cups vegetable stock (page 77) or water

1/2 head napa cabbage, cored and chopped

1   bunch watercress, tough stems trimmed

1/4 head green cabbage, cored and chopped

2   onions, chopped

1   stalk celery, chopped

3/4 teaspoon sea salt

1/2 teaspoon freshly ground black pepper

1/2 cup uncooked rolled oats

1/4 cup yellow miso

1/3 cup chopped fresh basil

Combine the stock, napa cabbage, watercress, green cabbage, onions, celery, salt, and pepper in a heavy stockpot. Cover and bring to a simmer over high heat. Decrease the heat to medium-low and simmer, stirring occasionally, for 10 minutes, or until the cabbage wilts. Stir in the oats, cover, and continue to simmer, stirring occasionally, for 12 minutes, or until the oats are very tender.

Using a handheld immersion blender, puree the soup in the pot until smooth. Alternatively, working in batches, puree in a regular blender until smooth. Remove the pot from the heat.

Prepared up to this point, the soup will keep for 1 day, covered and refrigerated. Before continuing, bring the soup to a simmer over medium-high heat, stirring occasionally.

Just before serving, rest a sieve atop the pot of hot soup, submerging the bottom of the sieve into the soup. Stir the miso in the sieve, dissolving it into the soup. Stir the soup to fully blend in the miso. Don't allow the soup to boil vigorously once the miso has been added, since doing so destroys some of the nutrients in the miso. Stir in the basil.

Ladle the soup into bowls and serve.

Curried yellow split pea soup

Everyone loves split pea soup. So I just played around with a traditional recipe by using yellow split peas instead of the standard green, and then upped the flavors with an exotic curry touch. This soup is even more delicious the day after it's made, since the spices have had more time to meld.

Combine the stock, split peas, bay leaf, and kombu in a heavy stockpot. Bring to a simmer over high heat, skimming off the foam that rises to the top. Decrease the heat to medium-low, cover, and simmer, stirring occasionally, for 45 minutes, or until the split peas are just tender and falling apart. Add the onion, celery, carrots, parsnip, squash, curry powder, salt, and cumin and return to a simmer over high heat. Decrease the heat to medium-low and simmer uncovered, stirring occasionally, for 40 minutes, or until the vegetables are tender and the soup is thick. Season to taste with more salt, if desired.

Ladle the soup into bowls. Sprinkle the mint over and serve.

The soup will keep for 2 days, covered and refrigerated. To rewarm, bring the soup to a simmer over medium heat, stirring occasionally and adding water to thin the soup to the desired consistency.

8	cups vegetable stock (page 77) or water
2	cups yellow split peas, picked through and rinsed
1	bay leaf
1	(2- to 3-inch) piece kombu
1	large onion, finely chopped
4	stalks celery, finely chopped
2	large carrots, peeled and finely chopped
1	large parsnip, peeled and finely chopped
1	cup diced seeded peeled butternut squash
1	tablespoon curry powder
2	teaspoons sea salt
1	teaspoon ground cumin
2	tablespoons thinly sliced fresh mint leaves

Creamy broccoli soup with red pepper crème

This is a very sophisticated soup because the roasted pepper crème makes a dramatic presentation and adds a deep, wonderful flavor.

2 tablespoons canola oil

2 onions, chopped

4 stalks celery, chopped

3 pounds broccoli, stems trimmed and coarsely chopped and florets cut into bite-size pieces

8 cups vegetable stock (page 77) or water

1 teaspoon sea salt

1/2 teaspoon freshly ground black pepper

3 cups packed fresh spinach leaves

1/2 cup Red Pepper Crème (recipe follows)

Heat the oil in a heavy stockpot over medium-high heat. Add the onions and celery, and sauté for 5 minutes, or until the onions are translucent. Add the broccoli stems and all but 4 cups of the florets. Sauté for 10 minutes, or until the vegetables are crisp-tender. Stir in the stock, salt, and pepper. Cover and bring to a simmer over high heat. Decrease the heat to medium-low and simmer for 20 minutes, or until the vegetables are very tender. Stir in the spinach.

Using a handheld immersion blender, puree the soup in the pot until smooth. Alternatively, working in batches, puree in a regular blender until smooth.

Add the reserved broccoli florets and return to a simmer over medium-high heat. Simmer for 8 minutes, or just until the broccoli florets are crisp-tender. Season to taste with more salt and pepper, if desired.

Ladle the soup into bowls. Drizzle the Red Pepper Crème decoratively over the soup and serve.

The soup will keep for 2 days, covered and refrigerated.

red pepper crème

Drizzle this roasted pepper crème into soups, but remember that a little goes a long way. I love it in the Creamy Broccoli Soup here, and with the Cream of Napa Cabbage and Watercress Soup with Basil (page 82).

Blend the roasted pepper, cashews, soymilk, lemon juice, and salt in a blender until smooth and creamy.

The crème will keep for 1 day, covered and refrigerated. Stir before using.

1   red bell pepper, roasted, peeled, and seeded (see below)

¹/₄ cup raw cashews

2   tablespoons unsweetened plain soymilk

1   tablespoon freshly squeezed lemon juice

¹/₂ teaspoon sea salt

ROASTING PEPPERS

Char any kind of peppers over a gas flame. Cooking time will vary depending on the size of the peppers. Most bell peppers will take about 5 to 7 minutes while chile peppers, like jalapeños, are often so small they will take only 2 to 3 minutes. Turn occasionally until the skin of the pepper blackens. Enclose the peppers in a paper bag and set aside until cool enough to handle. Peel and seed.

Lima bean and corn soup

A lovely soup year-round. It can be made in winter using organic frozen or canned corn, but it's also simply delicious without the corn. In summer months, when butternut squash isn't in season, skip the squash and add more carrots and corn.

2	cups dried baby lima beans, picked through and rinsed
1	(2- to 3-inch) piece kombu
12	cups vegetable stock (page 77) or water
1	bay leaf
1 1/2	teaspoons sea salt
2	tablespoons canola oil
1	large onion, chopped
4	stalks celery, cut into 1/3-inch pieces
2	carrots, peeled and cut into 1/2-inch pieces
1	cup diced seeded peeled butternut squash
2	tablespoons minced garlic
4	cups coarsely chopped green cabbage
1/2	cup yellow corn kernels (about 1 ear of corn)
1	tablespoon chopped fresh basil
1	tablespoon chopped fresh dill
1	tablespoon chopped fresh oregano
1/2	teaspoon freshly ground black pepper
1/3	cup yellow miso

Place the beans and kombu in a heavy stockpot. Add enough water to cover the beans by 3 inches. Let stand overnight. Drain and rinse the beans, reserving the kombu.

Return the soaked beans and kombu to the same pot and add the stock and bay leaf. Bring to a simmer over high heat, skimming off the foam that rises to the top. Decrease the heat to medium-low, cover, and simmer, stirring occasionally, for 25 minutes, or until the beans are just tender. Discard the kombu and stir in the salt.

Meanwhile, heat the oil in a large, heavy skillet over medium heat. Add the onion, celery, carrots, squash, and garlic. Sauté for 10 minutes, or until the vegetables are crisp-tender. Add the sautéed vegetables to the soup.

Stir in the cabbage, corn kernels, basil, dill, oregano, and pepper, and bring to a simmer over high heat. Decrease the heat to medium-low, cover, and simmer, stirring occasionally, for 15 minutes, or until the cabbage wilts and the flavors blend. Remove from the heat.

Prepared up to this point, the soup will keep for 1 day, covered and refrigerated. Before continuing, bring the soup to a simmer over medium-high, stirring occasionally.

Just before serving, rest a sieve atop the pot of hot soup, submerging the bottom of the sieve into the soup. Stir the miso in the sieve, dissolving it into the soup. Stir the soup to fully blend in the miso. Don't allow the soup to simmer once the miso has been added, since doing so destroys some of the nutrients in the miso. Season to taste with more salt, if desired.

Ladle the soup into bowls and serve.

Rustic Italian soup

I love this dish on cool-weather days. Serve it with hearty whole-grain bread and you've got a meal. This soup is a good example of how important it is to allow some time for flavors to meld. It becomes truly irresistible after the sage, kale, garlic, and tomato paste have simmered and joined flavors with the beans and the broth.

Place the beans and kombu in a heavy stockpot. Add enough water to cover the beans by 3 inches. Let stand overnight. Drain and rinse the beans, reserving the kombu.

Return the soaked beans and kombu to the same pot and add the stock. Bring to a simmer over high heat, skimming off the foam that rises to the top. Decrease the heat to medium-low, cover, and simmer, stirring occasionally, for 45 minutes, or until the beans are tender. Discard the kombu.

Blend 2 cups of the soup with the tomato paste and garlic in a blender until smooth. Stir the bean puree back into the soup, then stir in the kale, sage, salt, and pepper. Cover and bring to a simmer over high heat. Decrease the heat to medium-low and simmer, stirring occasionally, for 35 minutes, or until the kale is very tender and the flavors blend. Stir in the lemon juice.

Ladle the soup into bowls. Drizzle the olive oil over and serve.

The soup will keep for 2 days, covered and refrigerated.

2   cups dried kidney beans, picked through and rinsed

1   (2- to 3-inch) piece kombu

12 cups vegetable stock (page 77) or water

1/3 cup tomato paste

6   large cloves garlic

1   bunch kale, stemmed and chopped

2   tablespoons finely chopped fresh sage

1 1/2 teaspoons sea salt

1 1/2 teaspoons freshly ground black pepper

2   tablespoons freshly squeezed lemon juice (about 1 lemon)

4   teaspoons extra-virgin olive oil

Tarragon, tomato, and leek bisque

Remember growing up and eating countless cans of tomato soup? Everyone did it. I took that old standby to another level, making it a more grown-up soup—a thick bisque. Use a small potato that yields about 1 cup when chopped to get just the right consistency.

2   tablespoons canola oil

1   large onion, coarsely chopped

2   large leeks (white and pale green parts only), thinly sliced

1   small russet potato, peeled and coarsely chopped

3   cloves garlic, finely chopped

2   teaspoons sea salt

1/2   teaspoon freshly ground black pepper

1/8   teaspoon ground nutmeg

1/3   cup lightly packed chopped fresh tarragon

5   cups vegetable stock (page 77) or water

1   (28-ounce) can whole tomatoes

1   (6-ounce) can tomato paste

1   cup unsweetened plain soymilk

2   tablespoons finely chopped fresh Italian parsley

Tarragon sprigs, for garnish

Heat the oil in a heavy stockpot over medium heat. Add the onion, leeks, and potato. Sauté for 15 minutes, or until the onion and leeks are translucent and the potato is tender. Stir in the garlic, salt, black pepper, nutmeg, and 1/4 cup of the tarragon, then stir in the stock, the tomatoes with their juices, and the tomato paste. Return the soup to a simmer over high heat. Decrease the heat to medium-low and simmer gently, uncovered, for 15 minutes, or until the tomatoes are tender.

Using a handheld immersion blender, puree the soup in the pot until smooth. Alternatively, working in batches, puree in a regular blender until smooth. Stir in the soymilk, parsley, and the remaining chopped tarragon (about 1 1/2 tablespoons).

Ladle the soup into individual bowls. Garnish with the tarragon sprigs and serve.

The soup will keep for 2 days, covered and refrigerated.

Turkish lentil soup

Lentils and bulgur team up in this hearty and delicious soup. Look for medium-coarse bulgur at Middle Eastern markets and in the bulk section of natural foods stores. (Bulgur is often labeled according to its coarseness; in this case, a #3 grade will do.) If you use fine bulgur, the soup will be mushy.

Heat the olive oil in a heavy stockpot. Add the onions and sauté for 8 minutes, or until translucent. Stir in the garlic, rosemary, bay leaf, and cayenne pepper, and then the bulgur. Sauté over medium heat for 5 minutes, or until the bulgur is lightly toasted and the onions are golden brown. Squeeze the tomatoes into the bulgur mixture and add the juices from the can. Stir in the tomato paste, and then the stock and lentils. Bring to a simmer over high heat. Decrease the heat to medium-low, cover, and simmer, stirring occasionally, for 25 minutes, or until the lentils are just tender. Stir in the spinach, parsley, salt, and pepper. Simmer 2 minutes longer, or until the spinach wilts. Discard the bay leaf and season to taste with additional salt and pepper, if desired.

Ladle the soup into bowls and serve.

The soup will keep for 2 days, covered and refrigerated.

2	tablespoons olive oil
2	onions, chopped
6	cloves garlic, minced
2	tablespoons chopped fresh rosemary
1	bay leaf
$1/2$	teaspoon cayenne pepper
$1/2$	cup medium-coarse bulgur
1	($14^1/2$-ounce) can whole tomatoes
$1/4$	cup tomato paste
10	cups vegetable stock (page 77) or water
$1^3/4$	cups dried lentils, picked through and rinsed
4	cups lightly packed fresh spinach leaves (about 6 ounces)
$1/2$	cup chopped fresh parsley
$2^1/2$	teaspoons sea salt
$1/2$	teaspoon freshly ground black pepper

Tortilla soup

There are two basic types of tortilla soup: one is brothy, and the other is a heartier soup thickened with corn tortillas. I really love the second kind. Many of the folks working in my kitchens bragged about their hometown or family versions, so I set up a little contest to come up with the best tortilla soup. This hearty version came out the big winner. If you like a thinner soup, use fewer tortillas. And if you'd like to make this soup less spicy, cut away the veins and seeds from the jalapeño chile.

1	tablespoon canola oil
2	onions, coarsely chopped
3	cloves garlic, finely chopped
1	jalapeño chile, finely chopped
2	tablespoons tamari
2	teaspoons ground cumin
2	teaspoons sea salt
1	teaspoon dried oregano
1/2	teaspoon freshly ground black pepper
8	cups vegetable stock (page 77) or water
1	pound tomatoes, coarsely chopped
1/3	cup tomato paste
8	corn tortillas, coarsely chopped
1/4	cup finely chopped fresh cilantro
1/2	cup Crispy Tortilla Strips (page 106), for garnish
1	avocado, peeled, pitted, and cubed (optional)
1/2	cup Pico de Gallo (page 64), for garnish (optional)

Heat the oil in a heavy stockpot over medium heat. Add the onions and garlic, and sauté for 5 minutes, or until the onions are translucent. Add the jalapeño chile, tamari, cumin, salt, oregano, and pepper, and sauté 1 minute longer. Stir in the stock, tomatoes, and tomato paste. Cover and bring to a simmer over high heat. Decrease the heat to medium-low and simmer, stirring occasionally, for 10 minutes, or until the tomatoes are tender. Add the tortillas and simmer 10 minutes longer, or until the tortillas are falling apart.

Using a handheld immersion blender, blend the soup in the pot until smooth. Alternatively, working in batches, puree in a regular blender. Stir in the cilantro.

Ladle the soup into bowls. Garnish with the tortilla strips, avocado, and pico de gallo, and serve.

The soup will keep for 2 days, covered and refrigerated.

Salads and dressings

House salad with tahini-watercress dressing

On opening day at the very first RFD, I threw this dressing together and it became an instant hit (it's now RFD's "house" dressing). The watercress adds a slight hint of bitterness to the sweet of the tahini and the salt of the tamari. This dressing can be used on grain dishes, pressed salads, and—the most popular way at RFD—over the entire Real Food Meal.

To make the dressing: Blend all the ingredients together in a blender until smooth and creamy.

To make the salad: Combine the baby greens, cabbage, cucumber, carrots, and beet in a large bowl.

The dressing will keep for 2 days, covered and refrigerated. The undressed salad will keep for 8 hours, covered and refrigerated.

Just before serving, toss the salad with enough dressing to coat. Mound the salad in 4 wide, shallow bowls and serve immediately.

Tahini-Watercress Dressing

3/4	cup lightly packed watercress leaves (about 1 bunch)
1/3	cup roasted tahini
1/4	cup freshly squeezed lemon juice (about 2 lemons)
2	green onions (white and green parts), coarsely chopped
1	tablespoon tamari
1	tablespoon water
1	clove garlic

8	cups mixed baby greens
1	cup thinly sliced red cabbage
1	cup thinly sliced green cabbage
1	small unpeeled cucumber, cut into 1/2-inch cubes
2	carrots, peeled and shredded
1	beet, peeled and shredded

Caesar salad with blackened tempeh

Nori is a clever vegan substitute for anchovies and a key ingredient in this salad's dressing.

4 cups cubed whole-grain bread (³/4-inch cubes; about 3 large slices)

1 teaspoon crumbled dried rosemary

1 teaspoon dried basil

¹/4 teaspoon dried dill

¹/8 teaspoon freshly ground pepper

3 tablespoons olive oil

Caesar Dressing

2 ounces vacuum-packed extra-firm silken tofu

¹/3 cup freshly squeezed lemon juice (about 2 lemons)

¹/4 cup vegan mayonnaise

3 cloves garlic

2 teaspoons drained capers

2 teaspoons white miso

1¹/2 teaspoons nutritional yeast

¹/2 teaspoon sea salt

¹/4 teaspoon freshly ground black pepper

¹/2 of an 8-inch nori sheet, snipped into thin shreds

¹/3 cup extra-virgin olive oil

12 cups coarsely chopped hearts of romaine lettuce

2 cups Blackened Tempeh (recipe follows)

Preheat the oven to 375°F. Stir the bread cubes, rosemary, basil, dill, and pepper in a bowl. Drizzle the olive oil over and toss to coat. Spread the bread cubes in a single layer on a rimmed baking sheet. Bake, stirring occasionally to ensure even browning, for 20 minutes, or until golden brown. Cool completely.

To make the dressing: Combine the tofu, lemon juice, vegan mayonnaise, garlic, capers, miso, nutritional yeast, salt, and pepper in a blender. Sprinkle the nori into the mixture. Pulse once, then let stand for 5 minutes, or until the nori softens. With the blender running, gradually blend in the olive oil.

The dressing and croutons will keep for 2 days. Cover and refrigerate the dressing. Store the croutons in an airtight container at room temperature.

Toss the lettuce and croutons in a large bowl with enough dressing to coat. Mound the salad atop 4 large plates. Sprinkle the Blackened Tempeh over and serve immediately.

blackened tempeh

The title here is a little misleading since the tempeh is not "blackened" in the New Orleans way, in a skillet over high heat. It's baked, but the spicy coating has that Louisiana spirit. You're going to love this in salads, especially the Caesar Salad (opposite). I also like it with Mashed Parsnips and Potatoes (page 141) and served simply with Steamed Brown Rice (page 205).

$1/3$	cup canola oil
$1/3$	cup brown rice syrup
$1/4$	cup tamari
3	tablespoons plus 1 teaspoon paprika
2	teaspoons dried oregano
1	teaspoon dried thyme
1	teaspoon freshly ground black pepper
$3/4$	teaspoon ground cumin
$1/2$	teaspoon cayenne pepper
$1/2$	teaspoon garlic powder
$1/2$	teaspoon onion powder
12	ounces tempeh, cut into 4 by 1 by $1/2$-inch strips
2	tablespoons whole wheat flour

In a small rectangular pan, whisk the oil, rice syrup, tamari, 1 teaspoon of the paprika, 1 teaspoon of the oregano, $1/2$ teaspoon of the thyme, $1/2$ teaspoon of the black pepper, $1/2$ teaspoon of the cumin, $1/4$ teaspoon of the cayenne pepper, the garlic powder, and the onion powder. Add the tempeh and turn to coat. Cover and refrigerate overnight, turning occasionally.

Preheat the oven to 350°F. Line a heavy, rimmed baking sheet with aluminum foil. Lightly oil the foil. In a pie pan or shallow bowl, use a whisk to thoroughly blend the flour with the remaining spices: 3 tablespoons paprika, 1 teaspoon oregano, $1/2$ teaspoon thyme, $1/2$ teaspoon black pepper, $1/4$ teaspoon cumin, and $1/4$ teaspoon cayenne pepper. Remove the tempeh from the marinade, allowing the excess marinade to drip off. Add the tempeh to the flour mixture and turn to coat lightly. Arrange the tempeh in a single layer over the prepared baking sheet. Bake for 25 minutes, or until the coating is brown.

CAESAR SALAD WRAP

There's another great way to serve our Caesar salad: Wrap it up in a tortilla. This salad-on-the-go dish is delicious and convenient—and is the least messy way I know to enjoy a salad. Just spread a little Caesar dressing on the tortilla and roll the salad (with or without croutons) and blackened tempeh pieces in it.

Yin and yang salad with peanut-sesame dressing

The name of this salad is an homage to the ancient Chinese philosophy that all things in the universe contain elements of both yin and yang. Within each is the seed of the other, and when yin and yang work in harmony, all is good in the world. All is good in this salad, too. The crunchiness of the vegetables is the perfect counterpoint to the rich and creamy peanut dressing.

Toss the cabbage, carrots, radish, and green onions in a large bowl with enough dressing to coat. Mound the salad into 4 wide, shallow bowls or onto plates. Arrange the tofu around the salad. Sprinkle with the sesame seeds and serve.

4 cups shredded napa cabbage

3 cups shredded red cabbage

2 carrots, peeled and julienned

1 (2½-inch) piece daikon radish, peeled and julienned

10 green onions (white and green parts), julienned

1 cup Peanut-Sesame Dressing (recipe follows)

4 cups ½-inch cubes chilled Gingered Tofu (page 100)

2 tablespoons toasted sesame seeds (see page 41)

QUICK SOBA NOODLE SURPRISE

I used to eat hot noodles with peanut sauce at the cheap but fabulous Szechuan restaurants in Manhattan. I loved those dishes so much I would order two of them so I could take a whole order home and eat it cold the next day.

To assemble this dish, toss 4 cups of the Yin and Yang Salad (about one-fourth of the recipe) into a bowl with 1 pound of soba noodles, cooked, cooled, and tossed with 2 teaspoons of toasted sesame oil; add ½ cup cubed chilled Gingered Tofu cubes, pour in a generous amount of the peanut dressing, sprinkle with 2 tablespoons of toasted sesame seeds (see page 41), and you've got yourself a fantastic meal for you and three to five of your closest friends!

Cook the dried soba noodles just as you would cook dried linguine or spaghetti, and keep these three keys in mind when cooking any noodles or pasta: Use a large pot and plenty of water so the noodles have room to expand as they cook. Add the noodles to boiling water so they don't become gummy. And stir the noodles as they cook so they don't clump together.

Mexicali chop with crispy tortilla strips and lime-cilantro vinaigrette

The crunchy textures and flavorful ingredients make this a very satisfying main course salad. In a pinch, a 15-ounce can of drained organic pinto beans or black beans can substitute for the dried pinto beans. You can also substitute freshly squeezed orange juice for the lemon and lime juices in the vinaigrette.

1   cup dried pinto beans

1   (2- to 3-inch) piece kombu

6   cups water

Lime-Cilantro Vinaigrette

1/3   cup coarsely chopped red onion

1/4   cup freshly squeezed lime juice (about 3 limes)

1/4   cup freshly squeezed lemon juice (about 2 lemons)

2   tablespoons brown rice syrup

2   tablespoons brown rice vinegar

1   tablespoon ground coriander

2   teaspoons sea salt

1 1/2 teaspoons ground cumin

1/4   teaspoon cayenne pepper

1/2   cup extra-virgin olive oil

1/4   cup canola oil

1   cup lightly packed fresh cilantro

1   head romaine lettuce, thinly sliced

2   cucumbers, peeled, halved, seeded, and cut into 1/2-inch pieces

1   cup yellow corn kernels (about 2 ears of corn)

3   red bell peppers, roasted (see page 85), seeded, and cut into 1/2-inch pieces

6   stalks celery, cut into 1/2-inch pieces

2/3   cup finely chopped red onion

3   tomatoes, cut into 1/2-inch cubes

3   avocados, peeled, pitted, and cut into 1/2-inch cubes

2   cups Crispy Tortilla Strips (recipe follows)

Place the beans and the kombu in a large, heavy pot. Add enough water to cover by 3 inches. Let stand overnight. Drain and rinse the beans, reserving the kombu.

Return the soaked beans and kombu to the same pot and add the 6 cups of water. Bring to a boil over high heat, skimming off the foam that rises to the top. Decrease the heat to low, cover, and simmer gently, stirring occasionally, for about 1 hour. The beans should be tender but still hold their shape. Refrigerate the beans until cold, then cover and keep refrigerated. Drain the liquid before using.

To make the vinaigrette: Process the onion, lime and lemon juices, rice syrup, vinegar, coriander, salt, cumin, and cayenne pepper in a food processor or blender until smooth. With the machine running, gradually add the oils. Add the cilantro and process just until it is finely chopped. Season the vinaigrette to taste with more salt and cayenne pepper, if desired.

(continued)

The vinaigrette and cooked beans will keep for 2 days, covered separately and refrigerated. Whisk the vinaigrette before using.

Toss the lettuce, cucumbers, corn kernels, roasted bell peppers, celery, onion, and beans in a large bowl with enough vinaigrette to coat. Mound the salad in the center of large plates. Sprinkle the tomatoes, avocados, and tortilla strips over, and serve.

Makes 2 cups

crispy tortilla strips

1 tablespoon canola oil
6 (6-inch) corn tortillas
1 teaspoon blended chili powder
1/2 teaspoon maple crystals
1/4 teaspoon sea salt

These crisp strips of corn tortilla add a satisfying crunch to the Mexicali Chop. They also provide delicious texture as a garnish to the Tortilla Soup (page 90).

Preheat the oven to 350°F. Brush the oil over both sides of the tortillas. Cut the tortillas in half, then cut the halves crosswise into 1/8-inch-thick strips. Spread the tortilla strips on a heavy, rimmed baking sheet. Stir the chili powder, maple crystals, and salt in a small bowl to blend. Sprinkle the chili powder mixture through a sieve over the tortilla strips, toss the strips to coat, then arrange them evenly over the baking sheet. Bake, tossing occasionally, for 15 minutes, or until crisp. Transfer to a paper towel–lined plate and cool.

The tortilla strips will keep for 2 days in an airtight plastic bag at room temperature.

Corn and black bean salad

Serve this great little salad with any grain or noodle dish to make a wonderful high-protein meal. It's also a good accompaniment to a tossed salad. Use canned organic beans if you're in a hurry. One 15-ounce can yields 1¾ cups of drained beans.

Whisk the lemon juice, tamari, mustard, and pepper in a large bowl to blend. Gradually whisk in the olive oil to blend. Add the beans, corn kernels, bell pepper, green onions, and cilantro. Toss to coat.

The salad will keep for 1 day, covered and refrigerated. Toss again before serving.

¼ cup freshly squeezed lemon juice (about 2 lemons)

3 tablespoons tamari

2 tablespoons whole-grain mustard

¼ teaspoon freshly ground black pepper

3 tablespoons extra-virgin olive oil

1¾ cups drained cooked Black Beans (page 136), chilled

1 cup yellow corn kernels (about 2 ears of corn)

1 large red bell pepper, cut into ¼-inch pieces

10 green onions (white and green parts), thinly sliced

½ cup chopped fresh cilantro

Lemon-lime jicama slaw

This dish is absolutely incredible on the plate alongside our Seitan Tacos (page 155). The crisp, white, crunchy flesh of jicama is perfect for making crunchy slaws, but it's important to squeeze the shredded jicama to extract as much liquid as possible before combining it with other ingredients—otherwise the flavors will be diluted.

6   cups shredded peeled jicama (about 1 jicama)

1   teaspoon finely grated lemon zest

1   teaspoon finely grated lime zest

1/4   cup freshly squeezed lime juice (about 3 limes)

1   teaspoon sea salt

1/4   teaspoon freshly ground black pepper

Squeeze the shredded jicama to extract as much liquid as possible. Whisk the zests, lime juice, salt, and pepper in a large bowl. Add the jicama and toss to coat.

The slaw will keep for 1 day, covered and refrigerated. Toss the slaw again before serving.

Cherry tomato salad with tarragon and chives

This side salad is perfect alongside the Tofu Quiche with Leeks and Asparagus (page 158), and teams up beautifully with sandwiches.

Whisk the olive oil, vinegar, mustard, salt, and pepper in a large bowl to blend. Add the cherry tomatoes, teardrop tomatoes, shallots, chives, and tarragon, and toss to coat. Serve immediately.

2   tablespoons extra-virgin olive oil

2   tablespoons white wine vinegar

4   teaspoons Dijon mustard

$1/2$ teaspoon sea salt

$1/2$ teaspoon freshly ground black pepper

12   ounces cherry tomatoes, halved

12   ounces yellow teardrop tomatoes, halved

$1/4$ cup finely chopped shallots

2   tablespoons chopped fresh chives

2   teaspoons chopped fresh tarragon

Barbecued tofu chop with ranch dressing

People love chopped salads. The idea behind ours was to create a high-protein chop with originality, flavor, and texture. I think you'll agree that this salad stands up to any chopped salad. To make this salad during winter, when corn isn't at its peak, substitute blanched frozen green peas. It's important to pat the blanched vegetables dry; excess moisture can dilute the dressing or make the salad soggy.

Bring a large pot of water to a boil over high heat. Add the green beans and cook for 30 seconds. Add the carrots and cook 30 seconds longer, or until bright and crisp-tender. Drain the green beans and carrots and immediately place them in a bowl of ice water to cool. Drain again, and then pat dry (be sure they are very dry). Combine the green beans, carrots, celery, corn kernels, bell pepper, and onion in a bowl. The vegetables will keep for 1 day, covered and refrigerated.

Cut the warm tofu into 3/4-inch pieces. Toss the tofu with the barbecue sauce in another bowl to coat. Cover to keep warm and set aside.

Toss the lettuce in a large bowl with enough dressing to coat, and season to taste with salt and pepper. Mound the lettuce on plates. Toss the vegetables with enough dressing to coat, season to taste with salt and pepper, and mound them atop the lettuce. Scatter the tofu and cheese over the salad and serve.

4   ounces green beans, cut into 1/4-inch pieces

3   large carrots, peeled and cut into 1/4-inch pieces

4   stalks celery, cut into 1/4-inch pieces

1/2   cup yellow corn kernels (about 1 ear of corn)

1   red bell pepper, cut into 1/4-inch pieces

1   small red onion, finely chopped

6   slices Barbecued Tofu (page 131), warm

1/4   cup Hickory Barbecue Sauce (page 61), warm

8   cups chopped romaine lettuce

1 1/4 cups Ranch Dressing (recipe follows)

Sea salt and freshly ground black pepper

3/4   cup grated Cashew Cheddar Cheese (page 43)

Breads and spreads

Multi-grain quick bread

Though we classify dense and moist wheat-free bread as corn bread, it's nothing like traditional corn bread. It's based on a favorite recipe from Angelica Kitchen in New York but instead of the apple cider they use, I prefer apple juice, which gives it a sweeter taste. Make sure the brown rice, millet, and quinoa are cold before using them in this recipe or the mixture will be too soggy.

Preheat the oven to 375°F. Coat a 9 by 5¼ by 2-inch loaf pan with the 1 teaspoon oil. Combine the cornmeal, oats, and salt in a large bowl. Add the cooled brown rice and the millet and quinoa. Using your hands, mix the grains together. Stir in the apple juice and the remaining 3 tablespoons oil (the mixture will look soupy, but the grains will absorb the liquid as the bread bakes). Transfer the batter to the prepared pan.

Bake the bread for 1 hour and 30 minutes, or until it's firm to the touch and golden brown and cracked on top. Cool for 30 minutes in the pan, then carefully turn the bread out onto a wire rack. Slice and serve warm.

This bread is best the day it's made, but will keep for 1 day. Cool it completely, then store in an airtight container at room temperature. Wrap the bread in aluminum foil and rewarm it in a 350°F oven before serving.

3   tablespoons plus
    1 teaspoon canola oil

1¼ cups yellow cornmeal

1   cup old-fashioned oats

½   teaspoon sea salt

2½ cups freshly cooked
    Steamed Brown Rice
    (page 205), cold

1½ cups freshly cooked
    Steamed Toasted Millet
    and Quinoa (page 202),
    cold

3   cups apple juice

Sandwiches

Total Reuben with Thousand Island dressing

I started out serving our Reuben as an open-faced sandwich competing on the plate with mashed potatoes and gravy. Everyone loved the combo, but you felt like a lumberjack when you pushed away from the table. This updated version is lighter but every bit as satisfying. And for a gal who has never eaten a traditional Reuben sandwich—even after having lived in New York City for a decade—I still know a winning sandwich when I taste it. If you'd like to cut back on the fat even more, toast the bread without brushing it with oil, then spread the dressing and cheese over it. Stack with hot tempeh and sauerkraut.

To make the Reuben-style tempeh: Whisk the vinegar, rice syrup, tamari, coriander, caraway seeds, mustard seeds, and pepper in a large bowl to blend. Gradually whisk in the oil. Arrange the tempeh in a 13 by 9 by 2-inch baking pan. Pour the marinade over the tempeh. Cover and refrigerate at least 1 day and up to 2 days, turning the tempeh occasionally.

Preheat the broiler. Line a heavy, rimmed baking sheet with aluminum foil. Transfer the tempeh to the baking sheet in a single layer, reserving the marinade. Broil the tempeh for 5 minutes, or until golden brown on top. Turn the tempeh over and brush the top with the reserved marinade. Broil 5 minutes longer, or until golden on top.

To assemble the sandwiches: Spread 2 tablespoons of dressing over 1 side of 6 slices of bread. Place 1 slice of broiled tempeh atop each. Top the tempeh with the sauerkraut, dividing it equally among the sandwiches. Drizzle the remaining dressing over the sauerkraut. Spread the cheese over 1 side of the remaining 6 slices of bread. Place 1 slice of bread, cheese side down, atop each sandwich.

Lightly brush the oil over both sides of the sandwiches. Heat a large, heavy griddle over medium-high heat. Grill the sandwiches for 3 minutes on each side, or until heated through and golden brown. Cut the sandwiches in half and serve immediately.

Reuben-Style Tempeh

3/4 cup brown rice vinegar

1/2 cup brown rice syrup

1/2 cup tamari

2 teaspoons coriander seeds, coarsely crushed

1 teaspoon caraway seeds, coarsely crushed

1 teaspoon yellow mustard seeds

3/4 teaspoon coarsely ground black pepper

1/4 cup canola oil

3 (8-ounce) packages tempeh, halved horizontally

1 1/4 cups Thousand Island Dressing (recipe follows)

12 slices rye bread

3 cups drained sauerkraut

3/4 cup Tofu Ricotta Cheese (page 157)

1/4 cup canola oil

RFD burger

For years people suggested I serve a veggie burger, but I never wanted to enter that realm because of the gimmicky element involved. Tony Barone, our designer for the West Hollywood location, finally convinced me to create one. After several trials, we loved this tempeh and vegetable recipe more than any other. It's important that the tempeh and vegetables are both hot when mixed together. Gluten flour, different from bread flour and available at most natural foods stores, helps bind the mixture together. Be sure to sprinkle the flour on evenly so it doesn't clump but blends in uniformly.

Tempeh Patties

6	tablespoons canola oil
1 1/2	pounds tempeh
1/4	cup water
3	tablespoons tamari
2	tablespoons yellow miso
1 1/2	teaspoons sea salt
1	teaspoon freshly ground black pepper
3/4	cup gluten flour
1	portobello mushroom, stemmed and finely chopped
3/4	cup finely chopped red onion
3/4	cup fresh corn kernels (about 3 ears of corn)
3/4	cup shredded peeled beet
3/4	cup shredded peeled carrots
1/3	cup finely chopped green bell pepper
1/3	cup finely chopped red bell pepper
1	teaspoon minced garlic

3	tablespoons olive oil
2	large onions, cut into 1/2-inch-thick rings
	Sea salt and freshly ground black pepper
3/4	cup Homemade Ketchup (page 71) or organic ketchup
3/4	cup vegan mayonnaise
6	onion buns, split and toasted
12	strips Tempeh Bacon (optional; page 163)
6	romaine lettuce leaves
2	tomatoes, sliced

To make the patties: Preheat the oven to 350°F. Brush 1 tablespoon of the oil over a heavy, rimmed baking sheet. Shred the tempeh using a food processor fitted with the shredding disk or a hand grater.

Stir the water, tamari, miso, salt, pepper, and 3 tablespoons of the oil in a large bowl to blend. Stir in the tempeh. Sprinkle the flour evenly over the tempeh mixture and mix just until blended. Mound the tempeh mixture in the center of the prepared baking sheet. This will help to warm the tempeh mixture without browning or drying it out. Cover with aluminum foil and bake, stirring occasionally, for 20 minutes, or until the mixture is heated through.

Meanwhile, heat the remaining 2 tablespoons oil in a large, heavy skillet over medium heat. Add the mushroom, onion, corn, beet, carrots, bell peppers, and garlic. Sauté for 10 minutes, or until

(continued)

the vegetables are very tender. Add the hot sautéed vegetables to the hot baked tempeh mixture and stir to blend.

Working in batches, transfer the tempeh mixture to a food processor fitted with the metal chopping blade. Pulse just until blended (don't overblend or the mixture will become tough). Form the tempeh mixture into six 1/2-inch-thick patties. Wrap the patties with plastic wrap and refrigerate at least 4 hours and up to 2 days for the flavors to blend.

To cook and assemble the burgers: Heat 1 tablespoon of the olive oil in a large, heavy skillet over medium heat. Add the onions and sauté for 12 minutes, or until tender and beginning to brown. Season to taste with salt and pepper.

Meanwhile, heat the remaining 2 tablespoons olive oil on a large, heavy griddle. Sprinkle the patties with salt and pepper and grill for 4 minutes on each side, or until heated through and browned.

Spread the ketchup and vegan mayonnaise over the bottom halves of the toasted buns. Top each with a patty and 2 strips of bacon. Top with the sautéed onions, lettuce, and tomatoes. Place the bun tops on the burgers and serve.

Serves 4

The club

This double-decker sandwich flew out of the restaurant from day one. To this day it is still our most popular sandwich. Flakier and coarser than regular breadcrumbs, panko (Japanese breadcrumbs) create a terrific crunchy coating for the seitan.

Whisk the flour, arrowroot, sage, salt, thyme, pepper, and baking powder in a large bowl to blend. Whisk in the soymilk to form a smooth, thin batter.

Cut the seitan dough into 4-inch squares that are $1/3$ to $1/2$ inch thick. Dip the seitan squares into the batter to coat completely, then dip into the panko to coat. Arrange the coated seitan squares on a baking sheet. Cover and refrigerate at least 1 hour and up to 1 day.

Heat $1/2$ inch of oil in a large, heavy frying pan over medium-high heat. When the oil is hot, add the coated seitan squares and fry for $1 1/2$ minutes on each side, or until heated through, crisp, and golden brown. Using a metal spatula or tongs, transfer the seitan squares to a paper towel–lined plate to drain.

Spread the vegan mayonnaise over 1 side of each slice of toasted bread. Top 4 slices with the fried seitan and 2 slices of tempeh bacon. Top each sandwich with a second slice of toasted bread, another slice of tempeh bacon, avocado, tomato, and lettuce. Top each with a third slice of toasted bread, mayonnaise side down. Cut the sandwiches in quarter pieces and serve.

$1/2$ cup whole wheat pastry flour

$3/4$ teaspoon arrowroot

$1/2$ teaspoon rubbed dried sage

$1/2$ teaspoon sea salt

$1/4$ teaspoon dried thyme

$1/8$ teaspoon freshly ground black pepper

Pinch of baking powder

$1/2$ cup unsweetened plain soymilk

$1 1/4$ pounds Chicken-Style Seitan (page 175)

2 cups panko

Canola oil, for frying

$3/4$ cup vegan mayonnaise

12 slices sourdough bread, toasted

12 slices Tempeh Bacon (page 163)

1 firm but ripe avocado, peeled, pitted, and sliced

1 large tomato, thinly sliced

4 romaine lettuce leaves

Barbecue sandwich with barbecued tofu

To make attractive grill marks on this sandwich, cook the onions and tofu in the same spot on the grill pan or barbecue until the marks appear, about 2 to 3 minutes, then lift them up with a metal spatula and rotate them 90 degrees (don't turn them over yet). Continue cooking them until additional grill marks appear, then repeat on the other side.

1 tablespoon plus
1 teaspoon olive oil

6 ciabatta sandwich rolls
(about 4 inches in
diameter), split

3 medium onions, cut
into ¼-inch-thick rings

Sea salt and freshly ground
black pepper

1¼ cups Hickory Barbecue
Sauce (page 61), warm

6 slices Barbecued Tofu
(recipe follows), warm

¾ cup melted Cashew
Cheddar Cheese
(page 43), warm

2 tomatoes, thinly sliced

6 romaine lettuce leaves

Prepare a medium-hot fire in the grill or preheat a grill pan over medium-high heat. Brush the barbecue grill or grill pan with the 1 teaspoon olive oil. Grill the rolls cut side down for 2 minutes, or until heated through. Wrap the rolls with aluminum foil to keep them warm and set aside.

Brush the remaining 1 tablespoon olive oil over the onion rings. Lay the onions on the same hot grill or grill pan over medium-high heat and grill for 6 minutes on each side, or until the onions are tender and grill marks appear. Transfer to a bowl and season to taste with salt and pepper. Cover to keep them warm.

Spread some barbecue sauce over both cut sides of each sandwich roll. Place 1 barbecued tofu slice on the bottom half of each roll. Spoon some barbecue sauce and cheese over the tofu. Top with the grilled onions, tomatoes, lettuce, and the top half of the roll. Cut the sandwiches in half and serve.

barbecued tofu

Serve these barbecued tofu steaks in the Barbecue Sandwich, or cut them into pieces and serve them in a salad, such as the Barbecued Tofu Chop (page 111). They can also be served as an entrée accompanied by Corn on the Cob with Umeboshi (page 210), and the House Salad (page 95).

Drain the tofu and save the containers. Halve each piece of tofu horizontally, and pat dry with paper towels. Cover a baking sheet with more dry paper towels. Arrange the tofu slices in a single layer on the baking sheet and drain for 2 hours, changing the paper towels after 1 hour. Discard the damp paper towels.

Meanwhile, in a heavy saucepan, whisk the $1/3$ cup oil with the tamari, water, maple syrup, garlic, paprika, chili powder, maple crystals, thyme, cumin, curry powder, oregano, black pepper, mustard powder, and cayenne pepper to blend. Bring to a boil over medium-high heat. Decrease the heat to medium-low and simmer for 2 minutes. Cool the marinade slightly, then pour some of the marinade into each reserved tofu container. Place 1 tofu slice in each container. Pour more marinade over the tofu slices, and then repeat the layering with the remaining tofu slices and marinade. Cover and refrigerate at least 4 hours and up to 2 days.

Prepare a medium fire in the grill or preheat a grill pan over medium heat. Brush the barbecue grill or grill pan with the remaining 2 teaspoons oil. Grill the tofu, brushing with the remaining marinade, for 4 minutes on each side, or until the tofu is heated through and grill marks appear. Brush the warm barbecue sauce over the hot tofu and serve.

3   (14-ounce) containers water-packed firm tofu

$1/3$ cup plus 2 teaspoons canola oil

$1/2$ cup tamari

$1/4$ cup water

$1/4$ cup maple syrup

2   tablespoons minced garlic

2   tablespoons paprika

1   tablespoon blended chili powder

1   tablespoon maple crystals

$1 1/2$ teaspoons dried thyme

$1 1/2$ teaspoons ground cumin

1   teaspoon curry powder

1   teaspoon dried oregano

1   teaspoon freshly ground black pepper

1   teaspoon mustard powder

$1/2$ teaspoon cayenne pepper

$1/2$ cup Hickory Barbecue Sauce (page 61), warm

Grilled herb tofu sandwiches with sun-dried tomato pesto

The creamy pesto will keep for two days when covered and refrigerated. Reserve any leftover pesto to serve as a snack with crackers or toasted baguette slices.

Sun-Dried Tomato Pesto

2 cups water

1 1/2 cups sun-dried tomatoes (not packed in oil)

3/4 cup lightly packed fresh basil leaves

3/4 cup pine nuts, toasted (see page 41)

2 cloves garlic

1 teaspoon sea salt

1/4 teaspoon freshly ground black pepper

1/3 cup extra-virgin olive oil

1 tablespoon olive oil

2 red onions, cut into 1/2-inch-thick rings

Sea salt and freshly ground black pepper

8 slices hearty whole-grain bread, lightly toasted

4 slices Grilled Herb Tofu (opposite page)

3 cups chopped mixed baby greens

To make the pesto: Bring the water to a boil in a small saucepan over high heat. Add the tomatoes, cover, and set aside for 30 minutes, or until the tomatoes are tender. Drain the tomatoes, reserving the soaking liquid. Combine the tomatoes, basil, pine nuts, garlic, salt, and pepper in a food processor and blend until the tomatoes and basil are minced. With the machine running, gradually blend in the olive oil. Blend in about 3 tablespoons of the reserved soaking liquid to form a thick and creamy spread.

To assemble the sandwiches: Heat the olive oil in a large, heavy skillet over medium heat. Add the onions and sauté for 12 minutes, or until tender and beginning to brown. Remove from the heat and season to taste with salt and pepper.

Spread the pesto over 1 side of each of the bread slices. Place the grilled tofu atop 4 bread slices. Top with the warm sautéed onions, the baby greens, and the remaining bread slices, pesto side down. Cut the sandwiches in half and serve warm.

GRILLED HERB TOFU

There's something about the simplicity of tofu grilled with fresh herbs and garlic that puts this dish on my list of favorites. Be sure to use extra-firm tofu, which will hold its shape on the grill and not fall apart. Serve this in a sandwich, with grilled summer vegetables, or in the Green Noodle Roll (page 50).

Serves 4 to 6

2	(12-ounce) containers water-packed extra-firm tofu
1/2	cup extra-virgin olive oil
1/2	cup freshly squeezed lemon juice (about 3 lemons)
1/4	cup mirin
1/4	cup tamari
1/4	cup chopped fresh basil
1/4	cup chopped fresh parsley
1/4	cup minced garlic
2	tablespoons chopped fresh dill
1	tablespoon freshly ground black pepper

Drain the tofu and save the containers. Halve each piece horizontally, and pat dry with paper towels. Cover a large baking sheet with more dry paper towels. Place the tofu in a single layer on the baking sheet and let drain for 2 hours, changing the paper towels after 1 hour.

Whisk the olive oil, lemon juice, mirin, tamari, basil, parsley, garlic, dill, and pepper in a bowl to blend. Pour some of the marinade into each reserved tofu container. Place 1 tofu slice in each container. Pour more marinade over the tofu slices, then repeat the layering with the remaining tofu slices and marinade. Cover and refrigerate at least 4 hours and up to 1 day.

Prepare a medium-hot fire in the grill or preheat a grill pan over medium-high heat. Grill the tofu, brushing with the remaining marinade, for 4 minutes on each side, or until the tofu is heated through and grill marks appear. Alternatively, the tofu can be baked. To do so, preheat the oven to 400°F. Arrange the tofu on a baking sheet and bake for 10 minutes on each side, or until golden brown and heated through. Drizzle any remaining marinade over the tofu and serve.

The cooked tofu will keep for 1 day, covered and refrigerated.

Side dishes

Serves 6

Spanish rice

It's important to let the rice cook without stirring so the grains stay separate and fluffy. This popular rice is used in our burritos (pages 162 and 163) and served with our Seitan Tacos (page 155) and Black Bean Tostadas (page 165). It also makes a good accompaniment to other dishes, like the Seitan Fajitas (page 174) and Chorizo Tempeh Samosas (page 199).

Heat the olive oil in a large, heavy pot over medium heat. Add the onion, carrot, celery, bell peppers, jalapeño chile, and garlic. Sauté for 5 minutes, or until the vegetables are tender. Stir in the rice, and then the tomato paste, salt, cumin, and pepper. Add the water and the tomatoes with their juices. Bring to a boil over high heat. Decrease the heat to medium-low, cover, and simmer without stirring for 45 minutes, or until the rice is tender and the liquid is absorbed. Remove from the heat. Let stand, covered, for 10 minutes before serving.

Transfer the rice to a serving bowl. Using a fork, gently mix in the cilantro, and serve.

2 tablespoons olive oil

1 onion, finely chopped

1 carrot, peeled and finely diced

1 stalk celery, finely diced

1 green bell pepper, finely diced

1 red bell pepper, finely diced

1 jalapeño chile, seeded and finely chopped

4 cloves garlic, finely chopped

2 cups uncooked long-grain brown rice, rinsed well

2 tablespoons tomato paste

1 teaspoon sea salt

1/2 teaspoon ground cumin

1/4 teaspoon freshly ground black pepper

2 cups water

1 (14 1/2-ounce) can diced tomatoes

1/4 cup chopped fresh cilantro

Athena barley with kalamata olives and tomatoes

This versatile side dish is delicious served warm, at room temperature, or cold as a side salad with portobello mushrooms. Or make any of the phyllo appetizers (pages 55–58) an entrée by serving them with this dish.

Combine the water, barley, and salt in a large saucepan. Cover and bring to a boil over high heat. Decrease the heat to medium-low and simmer about 40 minutes, until tender. Transfer to a large bowl. If you're serving this dish as a cold salad, refrigerate the barley while preparing the remaining ingredients.

Whisk the lemon juice, olive oil, and oregano in a bowl to blend. Pour the vinaigrette over the barley and toss to coat. Add the tomatoes, olives, red onion, parsley, green onions, and dill and toss again to combine. Season to taste with salt and pepper and serve cold or at room temperature.

The salad will keep for 2 days, covered and refrigerated. Toss again before serving.

3 cups water

2 cups pearl barley

1 1/2 teaspoons sea salt

1/2 cup freshly squeezed lemon juice (about 3 lemons)

1/4 cup extra-virgin olive oil

1 tablespoon dried oregano

1 pound tomatoes, seeded and cut into 1/2-inch pieces

3/4 cup kalamata olives, pitted and quartered

3/4 cup finely diced red onion

3/4 cup finely chopped fresh Italian parsley

2/3 cup finely chopped green onions (white and green parts)

3 tablespoons chopped fresh dill

Freshly ground black pepper

Roasted spring and summer vegetables

These roasted vegetables make a delicious partner to any spring or summer entrée. Try them alongside Spinach Lasagna (page 156) or the Grilled Polenta and Vegetable Stacks (page 167). You can substitute other seasonal vegetables, such as asparagus and snow peas.

2 tablespoons olive oil

1/2 teaspoon sea salt

1/4 teaspoon freshly ground black pepper

2 yellow squash, halved crosswise and cut lengthwise into 1/2-inch-wide strips

1 zucchini, halved crosswise and cut lengthwise into 1/2-inch-wide strips

1 red bell pepper, cut into 1/2-inch-wide strips

3 ounces thin green beans, trimmed

1 small leek (white and pale green parts only), cut diagonally into 1-inch slices

1 teaspoon chopped fresh tarragon

1/2 teaspoon chopped fresh dill

Preheat the oven to 450°F. Whisk the olive oil, salt, and pepper in a large bowl to blend. Add the squash, zucchini, bell pepper, green beans, and leek, and toss to coat. Spread the vegetables evenly over a heavy, rimmed baking sheet, setting the bowl aside for reuse. Roast the vegetables for 20 minutes, or until tender, stirring after the first 10 minutes.

Return the vegetables to the bowl. Add the tarragon and dill and toss to coat. Season to taste with more salt and pepper, if desired, and serve.

Daily spring entrées

Sesame tempeh with sautéed collard greens and whole roasted garlic

Whole cloves of roasted garlic and crisp pieces of broiled tempeh intermingle with tender sautéed greens for one of my favorite southern dishes. Serve it with Mashed Yams (page 184) and corn bread (page 116). You can cook the tempeh and roasted garlic a day ahead, then add them to the hot greens and sauté just until heated through.

To make the tempeh: Cut the tempeh into 4 by 1 by $1/2$-inch strips. Whisk the tamari, maple syrup, sesame oil, mirin, ginger, and garlic in a 13 by 9 by 2-inch baking pan. Add the tempeh and turn to coat. Cover and refrigerate overnight, turning occasionally.

Preheat the broiler. Line a heavy, rimmed baking sheet with aluminum foil and brush with oil. Transfer the tempeh to the baking sheet, allowing the excess marinade to drip off, and arrange in a single layer. Reserve the marinade. Broil for 5 minutes, or until browned on top. Turn the tempeh over and brush with some of the reserved marinade. Broil 5 minutes longer, or until browned on top. Cut into 1-inch pieces and set aside.

To roast the garlic: Preheat the oven to 400°F. Place the whole garlic cloves in a small glass baking dish. Add the olive oil, salt, and pepper, and toss to coat. Cover the baking dish tightly with foil and bake for 30 minutes, or until the garlic is golden brown and tender. Cool and then peel the garlic, and transfer to a small bowl.

To make the greens and assemble the dish: Cut out the center vein from the greens. Cut the vein into 1-inch squares. Heat the oil in a large, heavy pot over medium heat. Add the onions, ginger, and minced garlic. Sauté for 5 minutes, or until the onions are translucent. Add 1 bunch of collard greens at a time and sauté each 2 to 3 minutes, until they begin to wilt, before adding another bunch. After adding the final bunch, cook 5 minutes longer, or until the greens are tender. Stir in the tamari, then the tempeh and roasted garlic. Sauté for another 2 minutes, or just until heated through.

Transfer to a bowl and serve immediately.

Sesame Tempeh

1	pound tempeh
$1/2$	cup tamari
2	tablespoons maple syrup
2	tablespoons toasted sesame oil
4	teaspoons mirin
$1 1/2$	teaspoons minced peeled fresh ginger
$1 1/2$	teaspoons minced garlic

Roasted Garlic

20	cloves garlic, unpeeled
2	tablespoons olive oil
$1/2$	teaspoon sea salt
$1/4$	teaspoon freshly ground black pepper

4	bunches collard greens
2	tablespoons canola oil
2	large onions, thinly sliced
1	(4-inch) piece ginger, peeled and cut into julienne strips
2	cloves garlic, minced
1	tablespoon tamari

Seitan enchiladas with salsa verde

Frying the tortillas briefly before filling them will not only make them pliable for rolling, it will also prevent them from becoming soggy after they're filled. If you're going to bake and serve the enchiladas immediately after rolling them, you can skip the step of frying the tortillas and instead just warm them briefly on a hot griddle. Serve these enchiladas with the Black Beans (page 136) and the Mexicali Rice (page 148) or Spanish Rice (page 135). If you'd like, drizzle a bit of Tofu Sour Cream (page 70) over the enchiladas before serving.

3 tablespoons olive oil

1 large white onion, finely chopped

1 jalapeño chile, finely chopped

3 large cloves garlic, minced

1 teaspoon sea salt

1/2 teaspoon ground cumin

1/4 teaspoon cayenne pepper

1/4 teaspoon freshly ground black pepper

1/2 cup vegetable stock (page 77) or water

4 cups Salsa Verde (recipe follows)

1 pound Basic Seitan (page 189), cut into 1/4-inch cubes

1/3 cup canola oil

12 (6-inch) corn tortillas

1/4 cup finely chopped fresh cilantro

Heat the olive oil in a large, heavy skillet over medium heat. Add the onion and sauté for 3 minutes. Add the jalapeño chile, garlic, salt, cumin, cayenne pepper, and black pepper and sauté for 3 minutes, or until the onion is tender. Stir in the stock and 1 cup of the salsa, and then add the seitan and toss to coat. Simmer for 5 minutes, or until the liquid evaporates.

Preheat the oven to 375°F. Pour 1 cup of the salsa into a 13 by 9 by 2-inch baking dish. Heat the canola oil in a small, heavy skillet over medium-high heat. Using tongs, briefly dip each tortilla in the oil for 15 seconds per side, or just until softened. Transfer to a paper towel–lined plate to drain. Place 1/3 cup of the seitan mixture in the center of 1 tortilla. Roll up the tortilla, then place the enchilada seam side down in the prepared baking dish. Repeat with the remaining tortillas and seitan mixture. Prepared up to this point, the enchiladas will keep for 1 day, covered and refrigerated.

Pour 1 cup salsa over the enchiladas. Bake until heated through, about 25 minutes. Sprinkle the cilantro over the enchiladas and serve with the remaining salsa alongside.

salsa verde

This is a traditional green version of salsa. This is great for dipping chips or serving over tostadas (page 165).

Combine the tomatillos, onion, jalapeño chile, salt, and pepper in a large, heavy saucepan over medium heat. Cover and bring to a boil. Reduce heat to medium-low and simmer for 15 minutes, or until the tomatillos are very tender. Add the cilantro and use a handheld immersion blender or a regular blender to blend until smooth. Season to taste with more salt and pepper, if desired.

- $1^1/_2$ pounds tomatillos, husked, rinsed, and coarsely chopped
- 1 white onion, coarsely chopped
- 1 jalapeño chile, coarsely chopped
- $3/_4$ teaspoon sea salt
- $1/_4$ teaspoon freshly ground black pepper
- 1 cup coarsely chopped fresh cilantro

CRUMBLED TOFU CHEDDAR

The tofu absorbs all the spices and seasonings to create a flavorful topping.

Makes $1^1/_2$ cups

- 8 ounces water-packed firm tofu, drained
- 2 tablespoons freshly squeezed lemon juice (about 1 lemon)
- 1 teaspoon curry powder
- 1 teaspoon dried thyme
- 1 teaspoon ground cumin
- 1 teaspoon sea salt
- $1/_2$ teaspoon turmeric
- $1/_8$ teaspoon freshly ground black pepper

Steam the tofu for 20 minutes, or until cooked through. Refrigerate until cold. Cut the tofu into $1/_8$-inch cubes. Whisk the lemon juice, curry powder, thyme, cumin, salt, turmeric, and pepper in a bowl to blend. Add the tofu and toss to coat.

The cheese will keep for 1 day, covered and refrigerated.

Seitan tacos

At the restaurant, we fry our taco shells and then fill them with the warm seitan mixture just before serving. If you have a taco shell fryer basket, you can deep-fry the tortillas in a pot of oil. But to ensure that most people can make the shells at home, the instructions below use cooking equipment found in most kitchens. Serve the tacos as an entrée with Lemon-Lime Jicama Slaw (page 108), Corn and Black Bean Salad (page 107), and Spanish Rice (page 135).

Heat 2 teaspoons of canola oil in a large, heavy saucepan over medium heat. Add the onion and bell peppers and sauté for 5 minutes, or until tender. Add the tomato, jalapeño chile, garlic, cumin, paprika, salt, and black pepper, and sauté for 5 minutes, or until the tomato is tender. Stir in the seitan and sauce, and simmer, stirring occasionally, for 5 minutes, or until the mixture is heated through and the flavors are well blended. Cool to room temperature.

Heat a griddle over medium-high heat. Cook a tortilla on the hot griddle about 10 seconds per side, or just until warm. Spoon 1/4 cup of the filling over the center of the tortilla. Fold the sides of the tortilla over the filling to form a taco. Secure the tortilla edges with a toothpick. Repeat with the remaining tortillas and filling. Prepared up to this point, the tacos will keep for 4 hours, covered and refrigerated.

Pour enough canola oil into a large, heavy frying pan to reach a depth of 1/2 inch and heat over medium heat. When the oil is hot, work in batches to fry the tacos about 1 minute per side, until crisp and golden. Transfer the tacos to a paper towel–lined plate to drain. Remove the toothpicks and fill the tacos with the lettuce and cheese. Serve immediately.

2 teaspoons canola oil, plus additional for frying

1 small onion, finely chopped

1/2 red bell pepper, finely chopped

1/2 green bell pepper, finely chopped

1 plum tomato, finely chopped

1/2 jalapeño chile, minced

2 cloves garlic, minced

1/2 teaspoon ground cumin

1/2 teaspoon paprika

1/2 teaspoon sea salt

1/4 teaspoon freshly ground black pepper

12 ounces Basic Seitan (page 189), cut into 1/4-inch cubes

3/4 cup Ranchero Sauce (page 67)

12 corn tortillas

3 cups shredded romaine lettuce

1 1/2 cups Crumbled Tofu Cheddar (page 153)

Spinach lasagna with herbed tomato sauce and tofu ricotta cheese

There's no need to precook the noodles for this lasagna. Just layer the dry noodles with the other ingredients, then cover the pan tightly to keep in all the steam during baking. Don't overcrowd the baking dish with too many dry noodles, though, because they expand as they cook.

2   tablespoons olive oil

2   onions, thinly sliced

6   cloves garlic, minced

2   teaspoons dried basil

2   teaspoons dried oregano

2   teaspoons sea salt

1/2   teaspoon freshly ground black pepper

12   ounces white button mushrooms, sliced

8   ounces carrots, peeled and thinly sliced

1   pound zucchini, thinly sliced

4   bunches fresh spinach, stems trimmed

2 3/4 cups Herbed Tomato Sauce (page 65)

10   eggless spinach lasagna noodles

3   cups Tofu Ricotta Cheese (recipe follows)

Heat 1 tablespoon of the olive oil in a large, heavy frying pan over medium-high heat. Add the onions, garlic, basil, oregano, salt, and pepper. Sauté for 5 minutes, or until the onions are tender. Add the mushrooms and sauté 8 minutes longer, or until the mushrooms are golden. Add the carrots and zucchini and sauté 10 minutes longer, or until the carrots are crisp-tender. Cool completely.

Meanwhile, steam the spinach: Pour enough water into a large pot to come 1 inch up the sides. Set a steamer basket in the pot, cover, and bring to a boil over high heat. Working in batches, loosely fill the steamer basket with spinach and steam 3 minutes, or until tender. Transfer the spinach to a bowl and, once all the spinach is steamed, cool, then squeeze to extract as much liquid as possible.

Preheat the oven to 350°F. Oil a 13 by 9 by 2-inch baking dish with the remaining 1 tablespoon olive oil. Spread 3/4 cup of the sauce over the bottom of the dish. Lay 3 noodles in a single layer atop the sauce (the noodles won't cover the bottom of the dish completely but will expand as they cook). Spread 1 cup of the cheese over the noodles. Cover the cheese with half of the sautéed vegetables and all of the spinach. Spread 1/2 cup of sauce over the spinach and top with 3 more noodles. Cover with the remaining sautéed vegetables. Spread another cup of cheese and then another 1/2 cup of sauce over the vegetables. Top with 4 more noodles to cover and spoon another 1/2 cup of sauce over the noodles.

Cover the pan tightly with aluminum foil. Bake for 1 hour, or until the sauce bubbles and the noodles are tender. Remove the foil and spread the remaining 1 cup cheese and then the final ¹/₂ cup sauce over the lasagna. Use a knife to swirl the sauce and cheese decoratively. Bake the lasagna 10 minutes longer, and then let stand for 15 minutes before serving.

Makes 3 cups

tofu ricotta cheese

When blended, the tofu gives this cheese a creamy consistency that resembles ricotta cheese. It spreads easily and works beautifully in lasagna, as well as on sandwiches like the Total Reuben (page 123), or layered between grilled polenta and vegetables, as in the Grilled Polenta and Vegetable Stacks (page 167).

14	ounces water-packed firm tofu, drained
²/₃	cup yellow miso
²/₃	cup water
¹/₂	cup tahini
¹/₄	cup extra-virgin olive oil
5	large cloves garlic
1¹/₂	teaspoons dried basil
1¹/₂	teaspoons dried oregano
³/₄	teaspoon sea salt

Blend all the ingredients in a food processor until smooth. The cheese will keep for 2 days, covered and refrigerated.

TOFU

I am adamant about using the right tofu in the right place. Water-packed tofu, also called "fresh" or "regular" tofu, is really better when it is meant to stand in for a major protein source. In that case, you'll need the firmness, strength, and density of water-packed tofu to hold its shape and take on flavor. In casseroles, quiches, and scrambles, as well as recipes that feature tofu on its own, water-packed tofu gives you the dimension you need for delicious, successful dishes.

I use the silken tofu, which is usually vacuum-packed, only for desserts and some light sauces and dips. This tofu, whether the soft or firm variety, produces that smooth, silky, creamy texture we all crave in our sweet endings.

Tofu quiche with leeks and asparagus

Firm tofu is blended into a creamy mixture and seasoned with garlic, oregano, thyme, and a bit of umeboshi to serve as the custard for this quiche. As the tofu mixture bakes, it sets up just like a traditional quiche. Serve this entrée for breakfast, brunch, lunch, or a light dinner alongside the Cherry Tomato Salad with Tarragon and Chives (page 109).

Crust

3/4 cup unbleached all-purpose flour

3/4 cup whole wheat pastry flour

1/2 teaspoon baking powder

1/2 teaspoon sea salt

1/4 cup canola oil

3 to 5 tablespoons water

Filling

12 ounces asparagus, trimmed

4 tablespoons olive oil

3 leeks (white and pale green parts only), thinly sliced

2 tablespoons minced garlic

4 teaspoons chopped fresh oregano

4 teaspoons chopped fresh thyme

1 3/4 pounds water-packed firm tofu, drained

3 tablespoons umeboshi paste

3/4 teaspoon sea salt

To make the crust: Position the rack in the bottom third of the oven and preheat the oven to 375°F. Blend the all-purpose flour, pastry flour, baking powder, and salt in a food processor. Pulse in the oil until the mixture resembles coarse meal, then mix in enough water to form moist clumps. Gather the dough into a ball, then flatten it into a disk. Press the dough into a 9-inch-diameter tart pan with a removable bottom.

To make the filling: Cut off the top 3 1/2 inches of the asparagus tips and set aside. Cut the lower portion of the asparagus stalks into thin slices. Heat 2 tablespoons of the olive oil in a large, heavy skillet over medium heat. Add the leeks, 1 tablespoon of the garlic, the sliced asparagus stalks, oregano, and thyme. Sauté for 8 minutes, or until the leeks are tender.

Meanwhile, bring a large pot of salted water to a boil. Add the asparagus tips and cook just until crisp-tender, about 2 minutes. Drain well and place on paper towels to drain further.

Blend the tofu, umeboshi paste, salt, and the remaining 2 tablespoons olive oil and 1 tablespoon garlic in a food processor until smooth and creamy. Transfer to a large bowl and stir in the leek mixture.

To assemble the quiche: Spread the tofu mixture over the prepared crust, mounding slightly in the center. Arrange the asparagus tips like the spokes of a wheel atop the filling, with the tips pointing toward the edge. Bake the quiche for 45 minutes, or until the filling is set and golden. Let stand 10 minutes. Cut into wedges and serve.

Stir-fried vegetables with steamed rice

I hesitated for years to put this dish on the menu because it seemed so common in vegan cooking. However, my guests kept asking for it, and now it's one of the more popular entrées. It's important to have the wok smoking hot before the vegetables are added so that they quickly become crisp-tender.

1/3 cup tamari

1/4 cup mirin

1/4 cup maple syrup

1   tablespoon plus
     1 teaspoon arrowroot

1   tablespoon yellow miso

1   tablespoon toasted
     sesame oil

3   tablespoons canola oil

1   tablespoon minced
     peeled fresh ginger

2   teaspoons finely
     chopped garlic

8   ounces broccoli florets

2   carrots, peeled and
     julienned

2   yellow squash, julienned

1   cup snow peas,
     julienned

8   fresh shiitake
     mushrooms, stemmed
     and thinly sliced

1/2 red bell pepper,
     julienned

1/2 head napa cabbage,
     shredded

4   green onions
     (white and green parts),
     julienned

4   cups Steamed Brown
     Rice (page 205)

Whisk the tamari, mirin, maple syrup, arrowroot, miso, and sesame oil in a bowl until well blended and smooth. Set the sauce aside.

Heat a large, heavy wok over high heat until very hot. Add the canola oil and swirl to coat the wok and heat the oil. Add the ginger and garlic and sauté for 10 seconds. Add the broccoli, carrots, squash, snow peas, mushrooms, and bell pepper. Pour the sauce over the vegetables and stir-fry for 5 minutes, or until the vegetables are crisp-tender and the sauce thickens slightly. Add the cabbage and green onions and stir to combine.

Transfer the vegetables to a large serving bowl and serve with the rice alongside.

Daily summer entrées

Grilled polenta and vegetable stacks with tomato-saffron coulis

Grilled polenta, portobello mushrooms, eggplant, and red onions are stacked with a creamy tofu cheese to make this impressive summertime entrée. Select an eggplant about four inches in diameter so the slices stack up nicely with the mushrooms and polenta. Serve with the Roasted Spring and Summer Vegetables (page 144).

To make the polenta: Combine the water, soymilk, olive oil, garlic, salt, and pepper in a large, heavy saucepan. Bring to a boil over medium-high heat. Gradually add the polenta, whisking until boiling and smooth. Decrease the heat to low and cook, whisking often, until the mixture is very thick, about 25 minutes (15 minutes for yellow cornmeal). Spread the hot polenta over a 13 by 9 by 2-inch baking dish and cool slightly. Cover and refrigerate at least 6 hours and up to 1 day. Using a 3¹/₂-inch-diameter cookie cutter, cut out 6 rounds of polenta. Reserve any remaining polenta for another use.

To grill the vegetables and polenta: Place the eggplant, onions, and mushrooms on a heavy, rimmed baking sheet. Generously coat with the vinaigrette and arrange them on the baking sheet with the mushrooms gill side up. Cover and marinate at least 1 hour at room temperature and up to 1 day in the refrigerator.

Prepare a medium-hot fire in the grill or preheat a grill pan over medium-high heat. Drain any excess marinade from the vegetables and sprinkle with salt and pepper. Grill, turning often, until tender, 8 minutes for the onions and 12 minutes for the mushrooms and eggplant. Grill the polenta until heated through, 5 minutes per side.

To assemble the stacks: Place 1 grilled polenta round in the center of each plate. Spoon 1 tablespoon of cheese over each polenta round and top with an eggplant slice. Spoon another tablespoon of cheese over the eggplant and top with the onions. Spoon 1 more generous tablespoon of cheese over each and top each with a mushroom, gill side down. Spoon the coulis around the stack and serve.

Polenta

3   cups water
3   cups plain soymilk
¹/₄ cup olive oil
3   cloves garlic, minced
2   teaspoons sea salt
Pinch of ground white pepper
2   cups polenta (coarse cornmeal) or yellow cornmeal

6   (¹/₂-inch-thick) slices eggplant
2   red onions, cut crosswise into ¹/₃-inch-thick rings
6   (4-inch-diameter) portobello mushrooms, stemmed
1   cup Balsamic Vinaigrette (page 124)
Sea salt and freshly ground black pepper
1¹/₄ cups Tofu Ricotta Cheese (page 157)
3   cups Tomato-Saffron Coulis (recipe follows), warmed

Sweet-and-sour tempeh with vegetables

Be sure to reserve the tempeh marinade; it's used later to enrich the sauce. Basmati Rice Pilaf with Roasted Peanuts and Cilantro (page 149) makes the perfect accompaniment, but Steamed Brown Rice (page 205) is delicious here, too.

1   cup tamari

1/4   cup water

3   tablespoons toasted sesame oil

5   cloves garlic, minced

1   tablespoon minced peeled fresh ginger

1   pound tempeh

1 1/4 cups maple syrup

1 1/4 cups brown rice vinegar

1/4   cup arrowroot

2   teaspoons crushed red pepper flakes

4   small onions, cut into 1/2-inch pieces

4   carrots, peeled, halved lengthwise, and cut crosswise into 1/2-inch pieces

3   stalks celery, cut crosswise into 1/2-inch pieces

1   red bell pepper, cut into 1/2-inch pieces

1   green bell pepper, cut into 1/2-inch pieces

1/2   head green cabbage, cored and cut into 1-inch squares

1 1/2 cups yellow corn kernels (about 3 ears of corn)

6   cups cooked rice

Whisk 1/2 cup of the tamari, the water, 2 tablespoons of the sesame oil, and the garlic and ginger in a 13 by 9 by 2-inch baking dish. Cut each tempeh square in half crosswise, then cut each piece in half horizontally. Place the tempeh in the marinade and turn to coat. Cover and marinate at least 1 hour at room temperature or up to 1 day in the refrigerator, turning occasionally.

Preheat the broiler and line a heavy, rimmed baking sheet with foil. Transfer the tempeh to the baking sheet, reserving the marinade. Broil for 5 minutes, or until golden brown on top. Turn the tempeh over and brush with the reserved marinade. Broil 5 minutes longer, or until golden on top. Cool slightly and cut into 1/2-inch squares.

Whisk the maple syrup, vinegar, arrowroot, and the remaining 1/2 cup tamari into the reserved marinade. Set the sweet-and-sour sauce aside.

Heat the remaining 1 tablespoon sesame oil and the crushed red pepper in a large, heavy frying pan with high sides or a large wok over high heat. Add the onions and sauté for 2 minutes, or until they begin to soften. Add the carrots and sauté for 2 minutes. Add the celery and sauté for 2 minutes. Add the bell peppers and sauté for 2 minutes. Add the cabbage and corn kernels, and sauté for 2 minutes. At this point the vegetables should be crisp-tender. Add the broiled tempeh, then stir in the sweet-and-sour sauce. Simmer, stirring occasionally, for 2 minutes, or until the flavors blend and the sauce thickens slightly.

Transfer to a bowl and serve with the rice.

Daily autumn entrées

Spicy tomato seitan stew

Thai flavors of lemongrass, kaffir lime leaves, and ginger blend seductively in this fragrant stewlike entrée. Kaffir lime leaves are available in the produce section of most Asian markets; lemongrass is available at natural foods stores, specialty markets, and some supermarkets. Serve the stew with the Confetti Jasmine Rice with Coconut (page 147) or Steamed Brown Rice (page 205) to soak up every last drop.

Heat the oil in a large, heavy skillet over medium heat. Add the onion, garlic, lemongrass, ginger, and serrano chiles, and sauté for 5 minutes, or until the onion is translucent. Add the bell pepper and sauté 3 minutes longer, or until crisp-tender. Drain the tomatoes and add to the stew, along with the tamari, vinegar, agave nectar, kaffir lime leaves, and salt. Simmer for 5 minutes, or until the tomatoes are very tender and falling apart. Stir in the seitan. Simmer for 5 minutes, or until the seitan is heated through, then stir in the basil.

Transfer the stew to a bowl and serve with the rice.

2   tablespoons canola oil

1   large onion, thinly sliced

3   tablespoons minced garlic

2   tablespoons minced lemongrass

2   tablespoons minced peeled fresh ginger

2   serrano chiles, thinly sliced into rounds

1   large red bell pepper, thinly sliced

1   (28-ounce) can whole tomatoes

1/4   cup tamari

2   tablespoons apple cider vinegar

1   tablespoon agave nectar

2   kaffir lime leaves

1   teaspoon sea salt

1   pound Basic Seitan (page 189), cut into 2 by 1/2 by 1/4-inch-thick strips

1/2   cup lightly packed fresh basil leaves

5 1/2 cups Confetti Jasmine Rice with Coconut (page 147)

Tempeh meat loaf

When making this dish, it's important that the tempeh and the vegetable mixture be hot when mixed together. Serve with the Mashed Parsnips and Potatoes (page 141), Golden Gravy (page 68), and Roasted Fall and Winter Vegetables (page 146).

Preheat the oven to 375°F. Lightly coat a heavy, rimmed baking sheet with 1 teaspoon of the canola oil. Shred the tempeh with a food processor fitted with the shredding disk or a hand grater. In a large bowl, stir the ketchup, miso, nutritional yeast, and soymilk to blend. Stir in the tempeh to coat, then sprinkle the flour evenly over and stir just until blended (the mixture will be moist). Transfer to the prepared baking sheet. Cover with foil and bake about 15 minutes, stirring occasionally to ensure even heating, until heated through.

Meanwhile, oil a 9 by 5 by 2³/₄-inch loaf pan with the sesame oil and set aside. Heat 1 tablespoon of the canola oil in a large, heavy skillet over medium heat. Add the onion, celery, carrot, and garlic. Sauté for 8 minutes, or until the vegetables are very tender. Add the tomato, oregano, rosemary, thyme, salt, and pepper. Sauté 5 minutes longer, or until the tomato breaks down. Add the hot tempeh mixture and stir to blend well.

Transfer the hot tempeh mixture to the prepared loaf pan and coat the top with the remaining 1 teaspoon canola oil. Cover and bake for 25 minutes, or until heated through. Uncover and continue baking 20 minutes longer, or until the top is golden brown. Cool for 5 minutes.

Invert the tempeh loaf onto a platter. Cut crosswise into thick slices and serve.

1	tablespoon plus 2 teaspoons canola oil
1¹/₂	pounds tempeh
¹/₃	cup Homemade Ketchup (page 71) or organic ketchup
¹/₃	cup yellow miso
¹/₄	cup nutritional yeast
2	tablespoons unsweetened plain soymilk
³/₄	cup gluten flour
1	teaspoon toasted sesame oil
1	cup finely chopped onion
¹/₂	cup finely chopped celery
¹/₂	cup finely chopped peeled carrot
2	teaspoons minced garlic
1	tomato, finely chopped
1	tablespoon finely chopped fresh oregano, or 1¹/₂ teaspoons dried
1	tablespoon finely chopped fresh rosemary, or 1¹/₂ teaspoons dried
2	teaspoons finely chopped fresh thyme, or 1 teaspoon dried
1	teaspoon sea salt
1	teaspoon freshly ground black pepper

Baked spelt macaroni with cashew cheddar cheese

Macaroni and cheese is a favorite of many children, and I think it's nice to offer it to them with a wheat-free noodle. Of course, any noodle will work just fine. The herbed breadcrumbs add a crunchy contrast to the creamy cheese sauce and tender macaroni. Corn on the Cob with Umeboshi (page 210) makes a good side dish.

12 ounces spelt elbow macaroni

2 1/4 cups melted Cashew Cheddar Cheese (page 43)

2 slices whole wheat bread

1 tablespoon chopped fresh Italian parsley

1 tablespoon olive oil

1 clove garlic, minced

1/2 teaspoon freshly ground black pepper

Preheat the oven to 325°F. Bring a large pot of salted water to a boil over high heat. Add the macaroni and cook, stirring often, for 8 minutes, or until tender but still firm to the bite. Drain, reserving 3/4 cup of the cooking liquid. Toss the macaroni with the melted cheese in a large bowl, adding enough reserved cooking liquid to moisten and coat the pasta. Transfer the macaroni mixture to an 8-inch square baking dish. Cover and bake for 20 minutes, or until heated through.

Meanwhile, chop the bread in a food processor until coarse crumbs form. Toss the breadcrumbs with the parsley, olive oil, garlic, and pepper in a bowl to coat. Uncover the hot macaroni and cheese and sprinkle the breadcrumb mixture over. Continue baking, uncovered, for 15 minutes, or until the topping is golden brown and crisp.

VEGAN CHEESE

Over the years, there have been several lines of nondairy cheese available, but most aren't completely vegan because they're made with casein, an animal by-product. But just because you're eating a vegan diet doesn't mean you have to miss out on integral parts of traditional dishes.

We've been serving great-tasting vegan cheeses at RFD for a long time. We've managed to find the right combination of ingredients to create a consistency, balance, and flavor very similar to a mild cheese. When we first introduced it on our menu, calling it a cheddar cheese, people flipped over it. Many also questioned our integrity. Rumors flew that we had lost our way, since folks thought we were serving real cheese. On one level, it was satisfying to know that people thought it was just like a flavorful dairy cheese. On the other hand, we had to spin the talk and continue to educate our guests about who we are.

Faux turkey breasts

Tempeh and tofu team up in these savory patties for a hearty and satisfying entrée that tastes great with the Mushroom Gravy (page 69). Shape the patties in your hand, allowing them to form against the contours of your palm to create natural-looking fillets.

1   pound tempeh

12   ounces water-packed firm tofu, drained

1/3   cup yellow miso

3   tablespoons Dijon mustard

1/4   cup plus 2 tablespoons canola oil

2   large onions, finely chopped

3   tablespoons Holiday Herb Mix (recipe follows)

1 1/2 teaspoons sea salt

1/2   teaspoon freshly ground black pepper

Using a food processor fitted with the shredding disk, shred the tempeh and tofu (the mixture will appear crumbled). In a small bowl, stir the miso and mustard to blend. Set the tempeh mixture and miso mixture aside.

Heat the 1/4 cup oil in a large, heavy frying pan over medium-high heat. Add the onions and sauté for 8 minutes, or until translucent. Stir in the herb mix, salt, and pepper, then stir in the tempeh and miso mixtures. Sauté for 8 minutes, or until golden brown. Set aside until cool enough to handle.

Preheat the oven to 350°F and brush 1 tablespoon of the oil over a heavy, rimmed baking sheet. Use your hands to shape the tempeh mixture into eight patties, using about 3/4 cup for each; make oval patties that are 4 to 5 inches long, about 3 inches wide, and tapered at 1 end to resemble chicken breasts. Arrange the patties on the prepared baking sheet and brush the remaining 1 tablespoon oil over the patties. Prepared up to this point, the patties will keep for 2 days, covered and refrigerated.

Bake for 35 minutes, or until golden and heated through.

holiday herb mix

This savory herb mixture is used in the Faux Turkey Breasts (opposite page) and the Corn-Sage Stuffing (page 180). Make a batch ahead of time so you can use it throughout the holiday season.

¹/₂	cup rubbed dried sage
¹/₄	cup dried marjoram
¹/₄	cup dried rosemary
¹/₄	cup dried thyme
1	teaspoon freshly ground black pepper

Stir all the ingredients in a small bowl to blend. Transfer the herbs to a glass jar with a lid.

The herb mixture will keep up to 1 month, stored airtight at room temperature.

THANKSGIVING

Because we close our restaurants every Thanksgiving Day, we prepare a nine-dish meal for takeout the day before. But months before the fourth Thursday in November, the calls start pouring in—hungry customers from all over want to make sure they can get our famous Thanksgiving dinner. Just like all Thanksgiving meals, ours is an elaborate and memorable production.

This meal was initially conceived on our first Thanksgiving in 1993, when a regular customer causally asked me to make him something for the holiday. I figured if I was going to make something for one person I might as well offer it to everyone. So, with only a few days before the big day, I whipped up a meal consisting of what I called "faux turkey breasts," yams, and my rendition of my family's traditional stuffing. I thought it was pretty good, and it covered the bases for Thanksgiving dinner.

Because of the great response I received, the next year I got serious and added more dishes to the meal, which now starts with soup and ends with pumpkin pie. We also began to advertise the meal ahead of time—and we had a deluge of orders. Year after year, this holiday event has grown, and we have standing orders with many customers.

Corn-sage stuffing

This is a special rendition of my family's holiday stuffing. Because of the cornmeal, the top is a bit crisper than the moist, white bread types, which means a delicious contrast of textures. Keep the simmering water with vegetables and herbs covered to prevent too much evaporation so you'll have enough liquid to moisten the stuffing.

1/4   cup plus 1 teaspoon canola oil

1   large onion, chopped

2   large cloves garlic, minced

8   stalks celery, finely chopped

4   carrots, peeled and finely chopped

3   tablespoons Holiday Herb Mix (page 179)

1   teaspoon sea salt

1   teaspoon freshly ground black pepper

1 1/2 cups water

3   tablespoons tamari

1   cup chopped fresh parsley

12   cups coarsely crumbled Southern-Style Skillet Corn Bread (page 116; about three-fourths of the bread)

Coat a 13 by 9 by 2-inch baking dish with 1 teaspoon oil. Heat the remaining 1/4 cup oil in a large, heavy pot over medium-high heat. Add the onion and garlic and sauté for 5 minutes, or until the onion is translucent. Stir in the celery, carrots, herb mix, salt, and pepper. Sauté for 5 minutes, or until the vegetables are crisp-tender. Stir in the water and tamari and bring to a simmer. Reduce the heat to medium-low, cover, and simmer, stirring occasionally, for 8 minutes, or until the vegetables are tender. Stir in the parsley.

Place the corn bread in a large bowl. Add the vegetable mixture, toss to coat, and transfer to the prepared baking dish. The stuffing can be made ahead up to this point. Cover with foil and refrigerate until ready to bake and serve.

Preheat the oven to 350°F. Bake the covered stuffing for 30 minutes, or until heated through. Uncover and continue baking 20 minutes longer, or until crisp on top.

Green bean casserole

Use a very sharp large knife or mandoline to cut the onions into very thin slices so the fried onion rings will be crisp and delicate. To be sure the oil is just the right temperature, use a deep-fry thermometer. The fried onions and boiled green beans can be made in advance, easing last-minute preparations.

Pour enough oil into a large, deep saucepan to reach a depth of 4 inches and bring to 350°F over medium heat. Whisk the flour, salt, and pepper in a large bowl to blend. Working in small batches, toss the onions in the flour mixture to coat lightly; shake off any excess flour. Fry the coated onions for 3 minutes, or until golden. Using a meshed or slotted spoon, transfer the fried onions to a paper towel–lined plate to drain. Season with additional salt.

Meanwhile, bring a large pot of salted water to a boil. Add the beans and cook for 3 minutes, or until just tender. Drain and cool completely. At this point, the fried onions and cooked beans will keep for 1 day. Store the fried onions in an airtight container at room temperature. Store the beans in a resealable plastic bag in the refrigerator.

Preheat the oven to 350°F. Toss the beans with the gravy in a large bowl to coat. Transfer the mixture to a 13 by 9 by 2-inch baking dish. Cover and bake for 30 minutes, or until the sauce and beans are heated through. Sprinkle the fried onions over and bake uncovered for 5 minutes, or just until the onions are crisp.

Vegetable oil, for deep-frying

1 cup unbleached all-purpose flour

1 1/2 teaspoons sea salt

1/2 teaspoon freshly ground black pepper

2 large onions, very thinly sliced into rings

1 pound fresh green beans, trimmed

2 cups Mushroom Gravy (page 69)

Mashed yams

Blend the yams in a food processor to get them ultra smooth and creamy. Feel free to adjust the maple syrup and spices to suit your taste.

6 pounds garnet yams, peeled and cut into 1-inch pieces

1/2 cup maple syrup

1/3 cup plain soymilk

2 teaspoons ground cinnamon

1/4 teaspoon ground allspice

Sea salt and freshly ground black pepper

Bring a large pot of water to a boil. Add the yams and cook for 20 minutes, or until tender. Drain, return the potatoes to the pot, and mash. Mix in the maple syrup, soymilk, cinnamon, and allspice. Season to taste with salt and pepper.

The yams will keep for 1 day, covered and refrigerated.

Cranberry relish

Here's a nice alternative to traditional cranberry sauces, which can be overly sweet. This retains a hint of tartness from the fresh cranberries—a perfect counterpoint to savory entrées. Don't worry about adding any liquid to the cranberries—as they cook, they release their own juices.

2 pounds fresh or frozen cranberries

1 teaspoon sea salt

1 cup maple syrup

2 tablespoons finely grated orange zest

Stir the cranberries and salt in a heavy saucepan over medium heat. Cook, stirring often, for 12 minutes, or until the cranberries release their juices, become soft, and have mostly fallen apart. Stir in the maple syrup and zest. Transfer to a bowl, cool, and then cover and refrigerate until cold.

The relish will keep for 5 days, covered and refrigerated.

Acorn squash stuffed with sweet rice, currants, and vegetables

By late summer, I just can't wait for the hearty winter squashes to come to market so I can make this dish. Use short-grain brown rice for the stuffing, since it stays tender even when cold. Serve this topped with Mushroom Gravy (page 69) or Golden Gravy (page 68).

Preheat the oven to 400°F. Cut a very thin slice off the rounded side of the squash halves to help them stand firmly on the plates and not topple over. Brush the inside of the squash with 1 tablespoon of the oil and sprinkle with salt and pepper. Arrange the squash bowls, hollow side up, on a large, heavy baking sheet. Roast for 45 minutes, or until the flesh is just tender. Keep the squash warm.

Meanwhile, combine the water, rice, and ¹/₂ teaspoon of salt in a 4¹/₄-quart pressure cooker. Lock the lid into place. Bring the pressure to high over high heat. Decrease the heat to medium-low and simmer for 15 minutes. Remove from the heat and let stand until the pressure reduces, about 10 minutes. Carefully remove the lid.

While the rice is cooking, heat the remaining 2 tablespoons oil in a large, heavy skillet over medium heat. Add the onion, celery, carrots, and oregano. Sauté for 12 minutes, or until the vegetables are tender. Stir in the tamari, then the currants and basil. Stir in the cooked rice and season to taste with salt and pepper.

Divide the rice mixture among the hot baked squash. Sprinkle the pepitas over the stuffing and serve.

The stuffed squash will keep for 1 day, covered and refrigerated.

4   small acorn squash (each about 12 to 14 ounces), halved lengthwise and seeded

3   tablespoons canola oil

Sea salt and freshly ground black pepper

3   cups water

2   cups uncooked short-grain brown rice, rinsed well

1   large onion, finely chopped

6   stalks celery, chopped

3   carrots, peeled and chopped

2   tablespoons chopped fresh oregano

2   tablespoons tamari

1   cup currants

³/₄   cup chopped fresh basil

1   cup pepitas, toasted (see page 41) and coarsely crumbled

SQUASHES

When I do my own personal grocery shopping at a local natural foods market, it's inevitable that while I'm in the produce section I am stopped and asked what to do with some exotic-looking vegetable that I'm inspecting. The person asking for help has no idea that I own the premier organic vegan restaurant in Los Angeles; what they see is a woman who seems to know what to do with these things.

Quite often, I am asked about winter squashes. People literally ask, "What do you *do* with that thing?" So I take the time to describe simply how to cut and bake or steam these squashes. Here is a quick rundown of my typical "Winter Squash 101" lecture.

Winter squashes are available all year, but their peak season is early fall to early winter. They have thick inedible skin, a hollow cavity, and very dense flesh that needs to be cooked longer than summer squash. Select squash that have dull-colored skin (shiny skin is an indication that the squash is not ripe) and a firm shell (avoid squash with damaged spots or cracks), and one that is heavy for its size. If purchasing a precut piece, select squash with darker flesh, an indication that it's riper. And as a bonus for my readers, here's a list of some of the most common varieties available:

- **Acorn**—dark green, ridged outer skin with deep yellow or orange flesh.
- **Butternut**—long and pear-shaped with tan skin and orange, sweet flesh.
- **Delicata**—this oblong-shaped squash's shell is cream-colored and green, and it's flesh is golden.
- **Golden nugget**—sometimes referred to as an Oriental pumpkin, this does in fact look like a small pumpkin in shape and color.
- **Hubbard**—a very large, winter squash with grainy-textured flesh. Shell is bumpy and ranges in color from dark green to orange.
- **Kabocha**—most weigh about three pounds and have spotted, dark green skin.
- **Pumpkin**—a very popular orange variety of squash from Halloween through the New Year.
- **Red Kuri**—a thick-skinned orange squash that looks like a smooth, oblong pumpkin.
- **Spaghetti**—when the flesh of this squash is cooked, it forms spaghetti-like strands with mild flavor.
- **Sweet dumpling**—small and plump with cream or light yellow coloring and green stripes.
- **Turban**—a small to medium-size colorful squash with a top that looks like a turban.

Daily winter entrées

Thai rice croquettes with udon noodles and peanut sauce

The list of flavorful spices and seasonings in these bite-size croquettes is long, but most of the work is in assembling and measuring them; the dish is easy to cook. The warm noodles are tossed with a spicy peanut dressing that doubles as a sauce here. The Orange-Glazed Tempeh Triangles (page 195) make a great accompaniment to this entrée.

Thai Rice Croquettes

2 1/2 cups water

1   teaspoon sea salt

2/3 cup uncooked sweet brown rice, rinsed well

2/3 cup uncooked short-grain brown rice, rinsed well

1/2 cup creamy peanut butter

3   tablespoons tamari

1 1/2 teaspoons ground ginger

1   teaspoon dried basil

1   teaspoon ground coriander

3/4 teaspoon ground cumin

3/4 teaspoon turmeric

1/4 teaspoon crushed red pepper flakes

1/4 teaspoon ground cinnamon

1/2 cup unsweetened shredded coconut, toasted (see page 41)

1   carrot, peeled and grated

1/4 cup minced fresh cilantro

1/4 cup minced fresh Italian parsley

2   green onions (white and green parts), minced

1/2 cup gluten flour

3   tablespoons canola oil (more if deep-frying)

9   ounces dried udon noodles

1 1/4 cups Peanut-Sesame Dressing (page 100)

To make the croquettes: Combine the water and 1/4 teaspoon of the salt in a large, heavy saucepan and bring to a boil over high heat. Add the sweet rice and short-grain rice, and return to a boil. Decrease the heat to low, cover, and simmer gently without stirring for 40 minutes, or until the rice is tender and the liquid is absorbed. Remove from the heat and let stand, covered, for 5 minutes. Transfer the rice to a bowl and cool completely.

Preheat the oven to 400°F. Lightly coat a heavy, rimmed baking sheet with oil. Stir the peanut butter, tamari, ginger, basil, coriander, cumin, turmeric, crushed red pepper, cinnamon, and the remaining 3/4 teaspoon salt in a large bowl to blend. Mix in the coconut, carrot, cilantro, parsley, and green onions. Stir in the cooled rice, sprinkle the gluten flour over, and mix. Using your hands, stir the rice mixture until it is well blended and the becomes sticky.

Using about 1 tablespoon for each, form the rice mixture into thirty 1-inch balls. Arrange the rice balls on the prepared baking sheet. Brush the balls with the oil and bake, turning occasionally, for 30 minutes, or until heated through and crisp. Alternatively, add oil to

(continued)

center of the potatoes, then wrap the potatoes around the filling to enclose completely. Roll in your palms to smooth the surface, then form the samosas into triangular shapes. Set the samosas in the prepared baking dish. Brush the remaining 1 teaspoon canola oil over the samosas. Prepared up to this point, the samosas will keep for 1 day, covered and refrigerated.

Bake for 35 minutes, or until heated through. Place 2 samosas on each plate, spoon the sauce over, and serve.

Makes 4 cups

1 tablespoon canola oil

1 large onion, thinly sliced

1 tablespoon minced garlic

1 tablespoon paprika

1 teaspoon sea salt

3/4 teaspoon ground cumin

1/4 teaspoon cayenne pepper

1/4 teaspoon freshly ground black pepper

1 (28-ounce) can whole tomatoes

1 1/4 cups vegetable stock (page 77) or water

spicy tomato sauce

A touch of cayenne pepper gives this sauce a little kick. Add more cayenne pepper if you'd like it spicier, or omit it completely for a mild sauce.

Heat the oil in a large, heavy saucepan over medium-high heat. Add the onion and cook, stirring often, for 5 minutes, or until translucent. Add the garlic and sauté for 2 minutes, then add the paprika, salt, cumin, cayenne pepper, and black pepper. Sauté for 1 minute, or until the spices are fragrant. Stir in the tomatoes with their juices and the stock and bring to a simmer over high heat. Decrease the heat to medium and cook, stirring occasionally, for 25 minutes, or until the tomatoes and onion are very tender. Season to taste with more salt, cayenne pepper, and black pepper, if desired.

The sauce will keep for 2 days, covered and refrigerated.

RFD meal

Steamed toasted millet and quinoa

These small grains are much lighter than rice and therefore the cooking time is shorter. Toasting the millet and quinoa before steaming them adds a rich, dark flavor, and adding the grains to the water after it comes to a boil makes them fluffier with less prone to clumping.

3/4   cup hulled millet
1/2   cup quinoa
2 1/2 cups water
1/2   teaspoon sea salt

Rinse the millet well and drain. Heat a large, heavy skillet over medium heat. Add the millet and stir constantly for 5 minutes, or until the moisture evaporates and the millet is fragrant, dry, and golden. Transfer the toasted millet to a bowl. Repeat with the quinoa.

Combine the water and the salt in a large, heavy saucepan and bring to a boil over high heat. Add the toasted millet and quinoa and return to a boil. Decrease the heat to medium-low, cover, and simmer gently without stirring for 25 minutes, or until the grains are tender. Fluff the grains gently with a fork and serve.

OUR DAILY FOOD

If a meal could serve as a metaphor, then this is it. Our Real Food Meal is the embodiment of all the nutritional approaches and philosophical principles that I have tried to follow during my lifetime.

This combination of healthful dishes best sums up how food attunes the body to its surroundings. Because it's best to eat with the seasons, this meal allows for a regularly changing selection of fresh, seasonal produce. The changing variety of grains, legumes, vegetables, and sea vegetables provides a wealth of nutrients, but it also creates the proper balance of colors, tastes, and textures on the plate.

You can eat all the components of the Real Food Meal at one time or create a meal around one, two, or three or more of its dishes. For instance, the Basic 3 (a vegetable, a grain, and a protein) is the favorite combination plate at the restaurants, and is a perfect mix of the kinds of food that you want to eat every day.

Serves 4 to 6

Arame with snow peas and carrots

We serve arame, a delicious sea vegetable, as a condiment on our Real Food plate. But you can also use hijiki, another sea vegetable that's very similar to arame. Since both are so rich in nutrients, you need only a small amount.

Rinse the arame in a strainer. Remove any grit or debris, then soak the arame in a large bowl of water for 10 minutes. Drain well.

Heat the sesame oil in a large, heavy skillet over medium heat. Add the onion and sauté for 8 minutes, or until tender and beginning to brown. Add the drained arame, carrot, 1 tablespoon of the tamari, and the mirin. Decrease the heat to medium-low and sauté for 8 minutes. Add the snow peas and continue sautéing until the vegetables are crisp-tender, about 4 minutes longer. Stir in the remaining 1 tablespoon tamari. Transfer to a bowl, sprinkle with the green onions and sesame seeds, and serve.

The arame will keep for 3 days, covered and refrigerated. Serve it warm, cold, or at room temperature.

1/2 ounce dried arame or hijiki

1 tablespoon toasted sesame oil

1 small onion, thinly sliced

1 large carrot, peeled and julienned

2 tablespoons tamari

1 tablespoon mirin

12 snow peas, quartered lengthwise

2 green onions (white and green parts), thinly sliced diagonally

1 tablespoon toasted sesame seeds (see page 41)

Black-eyed peas with kombu

Beans are making a big comeback. I happily notice them becoming accepted in our modern world as a serious plant-based protein food. And it's no wonder they're getting so popular: easy to prepare and delicious, they can be cooked with a wide range of herbs and spices and paired with a variety of cuisines. Almost any dried bean can be used in this recipe. Try adzuki, pinto, or navy beans in place of the black-eyed peas, but note that the cooking time will vary slightly depending on the type of bean you use.

2   cups dried black-eyed peas, picked through and rinsed

1   (1-inch) piece kombu

1   onion, chopped

1   small carrot, peeled and finely chopped

1/2   teaspoon sea salt

Place the beans and the kombu in a large, heavy pot. Add enough water to cover by 3 inches. Let stand overnight. Drain and rinse the beans, reserving the kombu.

Return the beans and kombu to the same pot and add the onion, carrot, and enough water to cover the beans by 1 inch (about 7 cups). Bring the water to a simmer over high heat, skimming off the foam that rises to the top. Decrease the heat to medium, cover, and simmer gently, stirring occasionally, for 1 hour, or until the beans are tender.

The beans will keep for 2 days. Cool, then cover and refrigerate.

Steamed brown rice

Eaten simply on its own or used in more elaborate dishes, brown rice is quick and easy to make and is a very nutritious staple to always have on hand. Brown rice takes nearly twice as long as white rice to cook, but it's more than twice as good for you. I generally find that if you put your pot of rice on first, by the time you finish making the rest of your meal the rice will be ready.

To cook in a pressure cooker: Combine the water, salt, and rice in a 4¼-quart pressure cooker. Lock the lid into place. Bring the pressure to high over high heat. Decrease the heat to medium-low and simmer for 40 minutes. Remove from the heat and let stand until the pressure reduces, about 5 to 15 minutes. Carefully remove the lid. Using a rice paddle, pull the rice away from the sides of the pot. Cover partially and let stand 5 minutes longer. Fluff the rice gently and serve.

To cook in a saucepan: Combine the water and salt in a large, heavy saucepan and bring to a boil over high heat. Add the rice and return to a boil. Decrease the heat to low, cover, and simmer gently without stirring for 40 minutes, or until the rice is tender and the liquid is absorbed. Remove from the heat and let stand, covered, for 5 minutes. Uncover and, using a fork, fluff the rice. Cover and let stand 5 minutes longer. Fluff the rice again and serve.

3 cups water

¼ teaspoon sea salt

2 cups uncooked short-grain brown rice, rinsed well

PRESSURE-COOKED BROWN RICE

Some home cooks still have an outdated image of pressure-cooking, dreading that the darn pot will blow up in their face. With today's pressure cookers, that fear won't be realized. More important, pressure-cooking is a terrific way to cook grains.

Pressure-cooking allows the heat to penetrate the outer covering of the grains, such as brown rice, softening it for easier digestion. Pressure cookers also have an uncanny ability to bring out the sweetness of whole grains.

When using a pressure cooker, be sure to allow enough time for the pressure inside the pot to reduce before removing the lid. If you don't, the steam that escapes as the lid is removed might burn you.

Steamed greens

Leafy greens are packed with vitamins and minerals. Eating them every day will give your skin a healthy glow. From collards and kale to mustard and turnip greens, keep a variety on hand to make this dish year-round. I also like cooking greens because it calls for using one of my favorite kitchen gadgets—a skimmer.

1	bunch collard greens, trimmed
1	head napa cabbage
2	teaspoons sea salt

Cut out the center vein of the collard greens. Cut the vein into $1/2$-inch pieces and set aside. Cut the collard leaves and cabbage leaves into 1-inch squares.

Bring a large pot of water to a boil over high heat. Add the salt and collard veins and boil for about 5 minutes. Add the collard leaves and, stirring occasionally, allow to boil for another 3 to 4 minutes longer. Add the cabbage and cook for 2 to 3 minutes, or until the cabbage and collard greens are tender. Using a skimmer, scoop up the greens and cabbage, allowing the excess water to drain back into the pot. Transfer the drained greens and cabbage to a bowl and serve.

Desserts

Pecan pie

I took my family recipe for pecan pie and replaced all the high-fat ingredients with more healthful ones. When flaxseed is used instead of oil, baked goods tend to brown more rapidly, so be vigilant during baking.

Position the rack in the bottom third of the oven and preheat the oven to 350°F. Whisk the maple syrup, rice syrup, and arrowroot in a heavy saucepan to blend, and bring to a boil over high heat. Decrease the heat to medium and simmer, stirring often, for 5 minutes. Pour the maple syrup mixture into a large bowl and set aside to cool to lukewarm.

Meanwhile, blend the soymilk, flaxseed, vanilla, and salt in a blender until smooth (the mixture will thicken as it blends). Whisk the soymilk mixture into the maple syrup mixture, then stir in the pecans.

Pour the pecan mixture into the baked crust. Bake for 40 minutes, or until the filling bubbles thickly and the crust is golden brown. Cool completely on a wire rack. Cut the pie into wedges and serve.

The pie will keep for 1 day, covered and refrigerated.

3/4 cup maple syrup

1/2 cup brown rice syrup

2 tablespoons arrowroot

1/2 cup plain soymilk

3 tablespoons ground flaxseed

1 teaspoon vanilla extract

1/4 teaspoon salt

2 cups pecan halves, lightly toasted (see page 41)

1 Oat Pastry Crust (page 227), baked

TOFU WHIP

This smooth nondairy topping is especially delicious with the Pecan Pie and Strawberry Kanten (page 225).

Makes about 2 cups

1/3 cup apple juice

1 tablespoon agar flakes

Pinch of salt

12 ounces vacuum-packed extra-firm silken tofu

1/4 cup maple syrup

1 teaspoon vanilla extract

Combine the juice, agar, and salt in a small, heavy saucepan. Bring to a simmer over high heat. Decrease the heat to medium-low, cover, and simmer, stirring frequently, for 15 minutes, or until the agar dissolves.

Meanwhile, blend the tofu, maple syrup, and vanilla in a food processor until very smooth and creamy. As soon as the agar is dissolved, pour the juice mixture through the feed tube with the food processor running, and blend into the tofu mixture until well combined.

Cover and refrigerate for 1 hour, or until set. Return the chilled tofu mixture to the food processor and blend until smooth and creamy

The tofu whip will keep for 2 days, covered and refrigerated. Whisk before using.

Peanut butter and jam cookies

For most of our baking at RFD, we use barley flour alone or in combination with oat and rice flour. These cookies are proof that you can make great-tasting baked goods without using wheat.

2 1/2 cups barley flour

2 1/4 cups oat flour

3/4 teaspoon baking soda

1/2 teaspoon sea salt

2 1/2 cups creamy peanut butter

1 3/4 cups maple syrup

1/4 cup canola oil

1/4 cup plain soymilk

1/2 cup raspberry preserves

Preheat the oven to 325°F. Line 2 heavy baking sheets with parchment paper. Stir the barley flour, oat flour, baking soda, and salt in a bowl to blend. Using an electric mixer, beat the peanut butter, maple syrup, oil, and soymilk in a large bowl to blend. Add the flour mixture and beat just until blended.

Using an ice cream scoop, scoop about 1/3 cup of dough for each cookie onto the prepared baking sheets, spacing 1 inch apart. Using the end of a wooden spoon, make an indentation about 1/2 inch in diameter that goes to, but not through, the bottom of each cookie. Spoon the preserves into a small resealable plastic bag. Using scissors, cut off 1 bottom corner of the bag. Use this homemade pastry bag to pipe the preserves into each indentation, mounding it just above the top of the cookie.

Bake for 22 minutes, or until the cookies puff and become pale golden. Set the baking sheet on a wire rack to cool.

The cookies will keep for 2 days, stored in an airtight container and at room temperature.

Chocolate chip cookies

An ice cream scoop helps form these wheat-free cookies quickly and easily and ensures that each is about the same size. If you find that the dough in this recipe or in the Peanut Butter and Jam Cookies (page 214) sticks too much to the ice cream scoop, lightly oil the inside of the scoop with canola oil to help the dough release more easily.

Preheat the oven to 375°F. Line a large, heavy baking sheet with parchment paper. Whisk the barley flour, oat flour, rice flour, and baking soda in a bowl to blend. Whisk the maple syrup, oil, date puree, rice syrup, soymilk, vanilla, and salt in a large bowl to blend. Add the flour mixture and stir just until moistened. Stir in the chocolate chips and the walnuts.

Using an ice cream scoop, scoop about $^1/_3$ cup of dough for each cookie onto the prepared baking sheet, spacing 1 inch apart. Flatten the cookies slightly. Bake for 18 minutes, or until the cookies puff, crack, and become golden brown.

Using a metal spatula, transfer the cookies to a wire rack to cool slightly. Serve warm or cool completely.

The cookies will keep for 2 days, stored in an airtight container and at room temperature.

1 $^3/_4$ cups barley flour

1 $^1/_3$ cups oat flour

$^3/_4$ cup brown rice flour

$^1/_2$ teaspoon baking soda

$^1/_2$ cup maple syrup

$^1/_3$ cup canola oil

$^1/_4$ cup date puree

3 tablespoons brown rice syrup

2 tablespoons plain soymilk

1 $^1/_2$ teaspoons vanilla extract

$^1/_2$ teaspoon sea salt

1 $^1/_4$ cups semisweet chocolate chips

$^3/_4$ cup walnuts, toasted (see page 41) and coarsely chopped (optional)

HOW TO MAKE YOUR OWN DATE PUREE

Simmer pitted dates in a saucepan of water until they are very tender. Using a slotted spoon, transfer the dates to a food processor and blend until smooth, adding some of the cooking liquid to moisten if necessary.

Double chocolate layer cake

You can turn this decadent double-layer cake into a four-layer cake by cutting each of the cake layers in half horizontally with a serrated knife and filling the extra layers with raspberry preserves. Serve with Tofu Whip (page 213) and/or Raspberry Puree (page 217) alongside.

3   cups barley flour

3/4   cup unsweetened cocoa powder

1/4   cup instant decaffeinated coffee powder

1 1/2   teaspoons baking powder

1 1/2   teaspoons baking soda

1   teaspoon sea salt

2   cups plain soymilk

1 1/2   cups maple syrup

3/4   cup canola oil

1   tablespoon apple cider vinegar

1 1/2   teaspoons vanilla extract

Chocolate Frosting

1 1/2   pounds vacuum-packed extra-firm silken tofu

1   cup unsweetened cocoa powder

1/3   cup agave nectar

2   teaspoons vanilla extract

2   cups semisweet chocolate chips

Preheat the oven to 325°F. Lightly oil two 9-inch-diameter cake pans with 1 1/2-inch-high sides. Line the bottom of the pans with parchment paper and lightly oil the paper. Whisk the flour, cocoa powder, coffee powder, baking powder, baking soda, and salt in a bowl to blend. In a separate large bowl, use an electric mixer to beat the soymilk, maple syrup, oil, vinegar, and vanilla. Mix in the dry ingredients just until blended.

Pour the batter into the prepared pans, dividing equally. Bake for 40 minutes, or until a toothpick inserted into the center of each cake comes out clean and the cakes begin to pull away from the sides of the pans. Cool in the pans on wire racks for 20 minutes, then turn out onto the racks and cool completely.

To make the frosting: Blend the tofu, cocoa powder, agave nectar, and vanilla in a food processor until smooth and creamy. Set aside. Stir the chocolate chips in a large metal bowl set over a saucepan of simmering water until the chocolate melts. Carefully add the melted chocolate to the food processor, then blend until thoroughly combined. Transfer the frosting to a bowl, cover, and refrigerate for 2 hours, or just until firm enough to spread.

Place 1 cake layer on a platter and spread 1 1/2 cups of frosting over the top. Top with the second cake layer. Using an icing spatula, spread the remaining frosting over the sides and top of the cake.

The cake will keep for 2 days. Cover it with a cake dome and refrigerate. Serve the cake cold or at room temperature.

Strawberry kanten

I call kanten a healthy person's Jello-O. As you might imagine, kids love this refreshing dessert. The only sweetener is apple juice, so be sure to select strawberries that are sweet, fresh, and at their peak. You can can deepen the berry flavor by using an all-natural apple-berry juice. And try substituting blueberries or raspberries for the strawberries.

Stir $1/4$ cup of the juice and the arrowroot in a small bowl to blend; set aside. Combine the agar and salt with the remaining 4 cups juice in a heavy saucepan and bring to a simmer over high heat. Decrease the heat to medium-low, cover, and simmer, stirring frequently, for 15 minutes, or until the agar dissolves. Whisk in the arrowroot mixture. Cover and simmer, stirring occasionally, over medium-high heat for 5 minutes. Stir in the vanilla. Transfer the kanten to a large bowl and allow to cool at room temperature. When just beginning to set, gently stir in the strawberries.

Spoon the kanten into dessert bowls, cover, and refrigerate for 4 hours, or until set.

The kanten will keep for 2 days, covered and refrigerated.

$4 1/4$ cups apple juice

1   tablespoon arrowroot

$1/4$ cup agar flakes

$1/8$ teaspoon salt

1   teaspoon vanilla extract

3   cups fresh strawberries (about 12 ounces), quartered

ARROWROOT

Always dissolve arrowroot in a cool liquid, such as water or fruit juice, before you add it to a recipe. It's also important to continue stirring the mixture—slowly, not vigorously—after you add the dissolved arrowroot. A few seconds after the mixture reaches a boil, it's cooked to capacity. In fact, arrowroot thins if cooked too long or stirred too much.